Bedtime Stories for Children

Relaxing Meditation Stories and Tales About Unicorns, Mermaids, Dragons, Princes, and Princesses to Help Your Toddler Achieve a State of Mindfulness and Fall Asleep Fast

© Copyright 2020

The contents of this book may not be reproduced, duplicated or transmitted without direct written permission from the author.

Under no circumstances will any legal responsibility or blame be held against the publisher for any reparation, damages, or monetary loss due to the information herein, either directly or indirectly.

Legal Notice:

This book is copyright protected. This is only for personal use. You cannot amend, distribute, sell, use, quote or paraphrase any part or the content within this book without the consent of the author.

Disclaimer Notice:

Please note the information contained within this document is for educational and entertainment purposes only. Every attempt has been made to provide accurate, up to date and reliable complete information. No warranties of any kind are expressed or implied. Readers acknowledge that the author is not engaging in the rendering of legal, financial, medical or professional advice. The content of this book has been derived from various sources. Please consult a licensed professional before attempting any techniques outlined in this book.

By reading this document, the reader agrees that under no circumstances are is the author responsible for any losses, direct or indirect, which are incurred as a result of the use of information contained within this document, including, but not limited to errors, omissions, or inaccuracies.

Contents

NOTE TO THE READER..1
NOTE TO THE LISTENER 2
CHAPTER 1: THE DRAGON THAT COUGHED..3
CHAPTER 2: THE PRINCE AND THE DRAGONFLY 6
CHAPTER 3: THE MERMAID'S LOST EARRING 11
CHAPTER 4: THE SHY UNICORN...15
CHAPTER 5: THE GIRL WHO LOVED MUSHROOMS 18
CHAPTER 6: THE BEAR WHO WAS TOO BIG 23
CHAPTER 7: THE PRINCE WHO WASN'T BRAVE.....................................26
CHAPTER 8: THE DRAGON WHISPERER 30
CHAPTER 9: A TALE OF THE BROKEN TAIL...36
CHAPTER 10: THE MEAN TWIN 41
CHAPTER 11: THE THREE NAUGHTY BROTHERS 47
CHAPTER 12: DRAGON BALL...51
CHAPTER 13: THE FISH THAT DANCED 56
CHAPTER 14: THE POOR BOY AND THE DRAGON.................................60
CHAPTER 15: REMINGTON THE SEAGULL 65
CHAPTER 16: THE MERMAID'S TEARS...68
CHAPTER 17: THE DRAGON ZOO 73

CHAPTER 18: THE ELF AND THE PRINCESS 79
CHAPTER 19: THE PLAIN PRINCESS 87
CHAPTER 20: THE LAST OF THE UNICORNS 94
HERE'S ANOTHER BOOK BY PEGGIE LANGSTON THAT YOU
MIGHT LIKE 99

Note To the Reader

This collection of children's stories is designed to help put your child into a quiet and meditative state that will facilitate peaceful sleep. Much will depend on how you read these tales and the attitude you have while you read them. We suggest that you encourage your child to lie on their back with their eyes closed and take a few deep breaths before you quietly read a story. At the end of each story, they should keep their eyes closed and breathe deeply half a dozen times to indicate that they want to hear more. Hopefully, they will nod off while you are reading and then enjoy a night of deep sleep.

Life is busy and demanding, and perhaps you would prefer to be taking a little well deserved "me" time, but remember these are precious times. In the mere blink of an eye, your child will have flown the nest, and you will look back on these moments with fondness, but also with an element of longing for that fleeting moment of innocence you are now enjoying. Wallow in it.

Few things are more important to a child's upbringing than reading and being read to. Hopefully, you will instill in them a passion for the printed word they will carry with them for the remainder of their lives. What you are doing now may seem small, but often it is our small inconspicuous acts with the most lasting effect.

Note To the Listener

You are about to go on an adventure, an adventure that will introduce you to faraway worlds and extraordinary creatures. There is no screen for you to watch. Most pictures you will draw with your imagination. To do this - to really meet the stars of each story - lie quietly with your eyes closed so they can visit you in the depths of your imagination. Lay back, close your eyes, take a few deep breaths and wait for your new friends to arrive and for the adventures to begin.

Chapter 1: The Dragon That Coughed

Long ago, in the remote mountains to the east, there lived many dragons. One was a very young dragon named Claude. Claude was the youngest of three dragons, and he longed to be like his older brothers. They were bigger, stronger, and braver than Claude. They also had one gift that Claude desperately longed for: they could breathe fire.

You need to understand that, for dragons, breathing fire is terribly important. It is, after all, the thing they are most famed for. Claude would spend hours trying to breathe a fierce, fiery breath he so longed to experience. Each attempt would end in failure, and worse, all that effort would make Claude cough.

His brothers, on the other hand, could summon up deep flames in an instant. The oldest could end some of these fiery displays with a chain of impressive-looking smoke rings that made him something of a hero amongst his friends. Of course, all of this fire breathing was not without problems. Once, one of Claude's brothers breathed fire indoors, which his mother had strictly ordered him not to do. The curtains caught fire, and if it were not for the quick reactions of their father, the whole house might have burned down. His brother was in trouble for weeks after that, but still, Claude remained envious. If only, he would think to himself, I could breathe just a little flame. It didn't have to be enormous or dangerous, just enough to prove that he really had the makings of a real dragon.

Day after day, he would wander into the mountains alone and try to force a flame to come from his mouth. Nothing. Not even a spark or a tiny wisp of smoke. All that effort was costing Claude dearly, and his coughing became worse, and his throat got sore. Also, he was sure that the other dragons were making fun of him behind his back.

He longed to play with his older brothers and their friends, but they always told him he was too young or that he was a nuisance. Even when his mother insisted they take him, they would sneak off when he wasn't looking, and he would find himself all alone again with his sore throat and his sad little cough.

One day, when his brothers had run off to play and had left him behind, Claude couldn't take it anymore, and he sat down on a rock and cried. Giant dragon tears rolled down his cheeks, and he wished he could make fire, but all he could make were tears.

When he looked up, he saw an old grandfather dragon nearby watching him.

"What is making you so sad, little dragon?" he asked.

"I want to breathe fire," sobbed Claude in short little breaths between each sob.

"And how have you been trying to breathe fire?" asked the old dragon.

"I have been huffing and puffing and breathing and wheezing, but all I do is cough."

"Mmm," replied the old dragon. "I think I see what the problem is. You are trying too hard. Let me help you."

"First, you need to relax. That is the most important thing. Why don't you lie down in the grass and close your eyes?"

Claude carefully climbed down from his rock and stretched out on the grass in the shade beneath a giant tree.

"That's good," said the old dragon. "Now, with your eyes closed, start to breathe deep and slowly."

Claude did as he was told.

"Good. Now, keep breathing but tell me what you feel. You must keep your eyes closed while you do this."

"I can feel the grass," said Claude, with his eyes gently closed.

"That's good. And what else?"

Claude needed to think for a moment.

"I can feel a slight breeze blowing."

"Excellent. And what can you hear?"

"I can hear the birds singing in the tree above me."

"You are good at this. Just keep your eyes closed and keep breathing and listen to the birds and feeling the wind and the grass."

Claude did what he was told, but the birds and the wind and the cool grass so soothed that he felt sleepy.

"Breathe deeply, little dragon." said his companion in that slow, deep voice of his.

Soon, Claude fell sound asleep. When he woke up, the old dragon was gone, and Claude was disappointed. He wondered if it had all been a dream.

He cleared his throat with a little cough and, as he did so, with no effort, a flame shot out of his mouth. Claude had finally learned how to breathe fire.

Sometimes, when we try too hard, things don't go the way we want them to. We need to relax and trust that all things will work out for the best.

Chapter 2: The Prince and the Dragonfly

Prince Oswald Leopold the Third was a very spoiled prince. Although he was just a boy, he could be very, very naughty. On bad days, he would pull his sister's hair, scare the palace cat, and was rude to the nursery maid. On good days, he was the charming young prince that one would expect from a boy who would one day be king.

Nobody was quite sure why Oswald had bad days. Even the young prince wasn't sure what suddenly made him want to be naughty. He just was. His parents, the king and queen, became desperate. They worried what would happen if somebody so naughty took over the throne. A naughty king is a terrible thing. Not only does he make himself unpopular, but he is also cruel to his people, and the whole kingdom suffers. In desperation, the king and queen sent Oswald to see every doctor in the land, but nobody could understand why the boy behaved so badly.

The king and queen tried different things. They punished Oswald, but that didn't work, so they tried bribing him by offering him a pony if he behaved. That worked for all of half a day, but then Oswald misbehaved again. On that particular occasion, he glued his two sister's pigtails together, and it took hours to pull the two princesses apart.

His bad behavior meant that Oswald had no friends. Normally somebody as important as a prince would have dozens of children to play with, but not Oswald. Parents would make excuses saying why they couldn't send their children to play at the palace. This upset the king and queen, but they had to admit that they couldn't blame them for keeping their children away from someone who could be both naughty and unkind.

This meant that Oswald spent a great deal of time playing in the palace gardens by himself. Even the princesses refused to have much to do with their brother. The young prince would pretend he didn't care he was alone, but truthfully, he was very lonely. He wished he could be nicer, but even though he tried, it was never long before he would find a cruel trick to play on someone. He was, he decided, just a bad person and he would have to accept it.

One day, as he was down by the big pond, he spotted a butterfly. There were many butterflies there, and he liked to trap them in his net and pull their wings off. It was, he realized, a cruel and terrible thing to do, but he did it anyway. He crouched down and tried to sneak up on the unfortunate creature, but as he did so, a dragonfly zoomed past his head, forcing him to duck.

Oswald was amazed at the creature's audacity. Didn't this insect know that he was a royal prince? He turned back toward the butterfly, but no sooner had he begun to stalk it than the dragonfly zoomed past him again, this time passing so close that Oswald was sure he would be hit in the eye. The prince was furious. He changed tactics. He would capture the dragonfly in his net and pull its wings off instead. He had never pulled the wings off a dragonfly, but he felt this one deserved it.

He looked around for his new target, and as he did, the dragonfly shot past him, brushing the top of his head as it flew by. Oswald had not even raised his net. A minute later, the dragonfly hovered just in front of the prince, but as Oswald lifted his net, the insect shot to one side and then back again, bouncing off his ear. It didn't hurt, but Oswald's pride was wounded. He wasn't used to being challenged, but that was exactly what the cheeky insect appeared to do.

The prince lifted his net and swung at the dragonfly, or rather at where the dragonfly had been. By then, the defiant creature was hovering just an inch in front of Oswald's nose, and he was sure it was making fun of him. Enraged, he took another wild swing, but the net never even came close to the agile dragonfly.

Oswald was getting more and more angry, and as he did, his swipes with the net were getting more and more desperate. Not once did he look like he might catch this insect tormenting him. After nearly an hour of swinging and swiping in the hot sun, Oswald was exhausted, and he sat down in the meadow. Immediately the dragonfly landed on a blade of grass just beyond his grasp. There the dragonfly calmy rubbed its eyes with its front feet in the way that dragonflies like to do. Oswald thought about taking one final swing at him but he was just too tired, so he lay back in the grass where he soon went to sleep.

Oswald would spend the rest of his life wondering if what happened next was real or just a dream. The dragonfly flew up into the air and then landed on the prince's ear.

"How dare you," he yelled. "Don't you know who I am? I am a royal prince and heir to the throne."

"To me, you are just a cruel little boy who likes to play mean tricks and pull the wings off of butterflies." said the dragonfly.

"I could have you put to death for talking to me like that," snapped the prince.

"Put to death," laughed the dragonfly. "You haven't done a very good job of that so far."

"I could have a hundred horsemen hunt you down," shouted Oswald.

"Really? And how is that going to look when a spoiled little prince comes home and orders a hundred horsemen to deal with one little dragonfly. Think of how much good that will do to the reputation of the future king."

Even in his rage, Oswald realized how stupid that would make him look. He didn't know what to say. It seemed that this silly little creature had gotten the better of him.

"Why are you so horrible, anyway?" the dragonfly asked when it became obvious the prince had nothing to say.

"I have good days, and I have bad days," snapped Oswald. "Today just happens to be a bad day."

"It seems to me that you have more bad days than good ones," said the insect.

Oswald knew the dragonfly was right, but he didn't want to admit it, and so he remained silent.

"Could it be that the bad days follow bad nights?" asked the dragonfly.

Oswald frowned. He hadn't thought about that.

"Well, I suppose it is possible," he said.

"I suspect that your bad days are a result of not getting enough sleep,"

Oswald thought for a moment, and it did seem that he could remember many nights where he had hardly slept.

"I can't help it if I don't sleep," he snapped.

"Of course you can, and it is up to you to try to sleep better. That way, you won't have bad days, and you might just find friends, so you don't need to be so cruel and nasty."

The prince thought about this for a while. He did wish he could stop having bad days, and he desperately wanted to have more friends.

"I don't see how I can just force myself to go to sleep."

"Well, I am going to teach you a trick. I want you to close your eyes and just relax."

The prince did as he was told, but he was sure that what the dragonfly was telling him wouldn't work.

"Now, with your eyes still closed, I want you to start to take slow deep breaths."

The prince thought this was silly, but he did it anyway.

It was an hour before the prince finally woke up from the deepest sleep he could ever remember having. There was no dragonfly, but the prince felt refreshed and happy for a change. He wondered if it was true and if lack of sleep was really behind all the bad days he had been having.

The prince slept much better after that, and the bad days stopped. He never saw the dragonfly again, but neither did he feel the need to pull the wings off butterflies, or scare the cat, or stick his sister's pigtails together. He would become a wonderful king; one who would always wonder if he had spoken to a dragonfly or just had a wonderful dream.

Chapter 3: The Mermaid's Lost Earring

Mindy was a very pretty mermaid who was the apple of her father's eye. He spoiled his little daughter, but at the same time, he remained very strict. One day for her birthday, her father gave Mindy a pair of very expensive and very beautiful earrings pearl earrings. Mindy loved those earrings more than any of her other possessions. The earrings came with strict instructions from her father, however. She was only to wear them on special occasions and not when she was out playing with her mermaid friends where they might get lost.

There were other rules that her father imposed that Mindy didn't like to follow. She was not allowed, for example, to play in the kelp forest. The kelp forest was a forest of tall seaweed just perfect for playing hide and seek in. The other mermaids often played there, but for Mindy, it was strictly forbidden.

It has to be said that sometimes Mindy did not follow all of her father's rules. She would occasionally sneak off and join her friends for a few hours in the kelp forest. There were even times when Mindy played in the kelp forest while wearing her beloved earrings.

The kelp forest was a strange and eerie place. It was filled with shadows, rock caves, and other dark and spooky places. Her friends all loved to play there, in part because it was so scary. It was also the place where Leroy the moray eel lived. Leroy was a long black eel with dark blue spots and a huge mouth filled with needle-like teeth. The mermaids hardly ever saw Leroy, but they were all terrified of him. The fact that he was lurking there, somewhere in the dark, made the kelp forest much more exciting.

Once, Mindy and her friends played a game of tag in the kelp forest, and soon they were all chasing each other backward and forward through the shadows. They lost all track of time until suddenly they realized that it was later than they thought, and they realized they had better be getting home. As they gathered to wish one another a quick farewell, one mermaid looked at Mindy and said, "Where is your earring? You only have one."

Mindy's hand flew to her ear, and sure enough, her friend was right. One of the beloved earrings was gone. She felt her stomach turn. On the one hand, she was terrified because she knew she would be in big trouble, but she was also heartbroken because she loved those earrings so much.

"Come and help me search for it," she wailed desperately. Her friends wanted to help her, but because it was so late, they couldn't. They all knew they would be in trouble if they didn't get home soon.

Finally, Mindy had no choice but to turn and swim back into the kelp forest by herself. The forest was a different place now that she was alone. What's more, it was getting late, and as the light began to fade, the shadows grew longer, and everything began to become far more sinister.

Mindy forced herself to keep going, even though she was desperate to turn around and swim home where her dinner would be waiting, and she would be safe in the arms of her family. Several times she thought about giving up, but she just couldn't face having to tell her father she had lost one of the earrings he had given her - one of the earrings she had been told not to wear. What's more, she would have to confess that it had been lost in the kelp forest where she knew she was not allowed to play.

Mindy swam among the giant stems of kelp, but there was no sign of the precious earring. It was growing darker, and she realized that if she didn't turn around and head for home soon, she might get lost. Suddenly she saw a dark shadow gliding through the forest below her. Could it be the moray eel Leroy, who all the children were so scared of? The shadow vanished, and Mindy wondered if had she imagined it.

Just the thought of Leroy made her frightened, and she was scared enough already. She decided that she would give up and go home. If she were lucky, she decided, her father wouldn't notice the earring was missing, and she could sneak back to the forest the next day and search again. There would be more daylight, and perhaps some of her friends would help her.

As she made her way out of the forest, she kept nervously glancing over her shoulder to check that Leroy wasn't following her. She was nearly out of the forest where it was a little less dark when suddenly, the ugly moray eel appeared. She had heard so much about Leroy but had never seen him, and now he was here right in front of her. He was even uglier and more frightening than Mindy had imagined he would be. His face was fierce, and the thick skin around his neck was leathery and wrinkled. Worst of all, his mouth was filled with rows of long sharp teeth. Mindy was convinced that she was about to be eaten alive when Leroy spoke.

"Have you lost an earring by any chance, little mermaid?" he asked.

Mindy was so frightened that she couldn't speak. All she could manage was a brief nod of her head.

"Follow me," said Leroy. 'I'll show you where you dropped it."

Mindy wasn't sure about all of this. Could this be some kind of a trap to lead her back into the kelp forest and harm her?

Leroy looked at her and then spoke again. "I know you children are afraid of me. It is because I am so ugly. There is not much I can do about that. It does mean that I am terribly lonely, though. That is why I hide when you children come to play in the kelp forest. I don't like to frighten you, but I do enjoy having you there. I don't hear much laughter when I am all alone."

Mindy didn't know what to say. Suddenly she felt sorry for the ugly old eel, and he didn't seem so terrifying anymore. She followed him back into the forest, where he quickly showed her the earring lying on a patch of sand on the seabed.

When she had put it back on, he spoke again. "It is getting dark. I think I'd better lead you out of the forest, so you don't get lost." He swam ahead of her and quickly led the little mermaid out of the forest.

"I don't know how to thank you," she said as they reached the forest edge.

"Don't you mention it, young lady. I am just glad that I could help."

Mindy started to swim for home, but then she had an idea and turned back.

"Leroy," she said, "if my friends and I are back here tomorrow or the next day, would it be okay if we dropped in and visited you?"

Suddenly the old eel had tears in his eyes.

"Young lady," he said in a slightly husky voice, "nothing would make me happier."

Later that night, as she lay in bed, Mindy felt herself drifting off to sleep, and she had a smile on her face as she did so. Wouldn't her friends be surprised when she introduced them to her new friend!

Chapter 4: The Shy Unicorn

Miranda had heard about Unicorns, but she had never seen one. In fact, she wasn't even sure if they really existed or if they were a story that old people had made up to entertain her. One day, she wandered out into the forest looking for mushrooms. While she was there, she heard a rustle in the bushes and looked up to see a small pony-like creature dashing off into the shadows. It was pure white, and she was sure she had seen a horn growing on his head.

She told herself she must be imaging things and that it was just a white pony. She only got a brief glimpse of the animal, but already Miranda was very excited. She chased him through the forest, and although she only caught occasional glimpses of him, she never got close. In her excitement, Miranda lost all track of time and, when she eventually stopped to catch her breath, she suddenly realized that she was lost.

Frightened, she tried to find her way back through the woods. Soon, she realized that she had no idea where she was. She wandered backward and forward, looking for a familiar tree or path that would help guide her home. It was soon clear that Miranda had wandered into a new part of the woods she didn't know. To make matters worse, it was getting dark, and Miranda got even more scared. Around and around she walked, but she was getting no closer to finding a way home. She became so afraid that she knelt down in a small clearing and cried.

The little girl had no idea where she was or what she should do. She just kneeled in the grass and sobbed. Suddenly, she heard a noise beside her and looked up to see a small white creature standing beneath a tree looking at her. This time she could see it clearly, and there was no doubt that what she was seeing was a baby unicorn.

"Who are you?" she asked.

"My name is Walter," he said shyly.

"You are a unicorn," she said with shock.

"Yes, I am," said the small, shy creature. "Why are you crying?"

"I was trying to catch you, and I became lost," said Miranda

"Why were you trying to catch me?"

"I just wanted to talk to you. I wasn't sure if unicorns really existed, you see. We hear so much about you, but I thought it might just have been a story my parents made up."

"There are still a few of us living here in the forest," said Walter, "but there are not many of us anymore."

"Well, why do we never see you then?" Miranda wanted to know.

"We unicorns are very afraid of the humans," said Walter.

"But why would you be afraid of humans?" Miranda asked.

"There used to be many of us," said Walter, "but long ago, humans started to hunt us. They thought that our horns were magical. Many of my ancestors were killed just because people wanted our horns."

Miranda thought about this for a moment. She vaguely remembered people saying the unicorn horns were magical, but she couldn't imagine harming such a beautiful animal.

"If that is the case," she said, "then why are you here talking to me?"

"Well, I couldn't bear to hear you crying and looking so sad."

"I'm sorry," she replied, feeling embarrassed. "I wanted to get a better look at you, and so I tried to follow you and became terribly lost. I hope I didn't scare you."

"That's okay," said Walter. "Would you like me to guide you back to the edge of the woods?"

Together, Miranda and Walter wound their way back through the forest. Along the way, they chatted about their lives and how different they were. Both realized that though their worlds were very different, they still had a lot in common and could easily become friends.

When they reached the edge of the woods, and Miranda once more knew where she was, the pair parted company. Before they did so, however, they agreed to meet the following week. Walter also made Miranda promise never to tell any other humans she had seen a unicorn. It would, he told her, make his life very dangerous if people realized unicorns still lived in the woods.

When Miranda got home, she was in trouble for being so late. It was already dark by then, and both her parents had been worried about her. She was sent to bed straight after dinner, but her mother and father loved her very much, and they couldn't stay angry at her for long. Before she dropped off to sleep, her mother crept into her room and asked if Miranda would like to hear a quick story.

"Yes, please," said the sleepy girl. "Could you tell me one about unicorns?"

As her mother told her a story, Miranda closed her eyes and listened. It was a story she had heard many times before, but she didn't mind. She no longer needed to imagine what a unicorn looked like. She had made friends with one, and though she couldn't tell her mother, as she lay there with her eyes closed, she was thinking of Walter and the fun they would have the following week.

Chapter 5: The Girl Who Loved Mushrooms

Belinda Birtwistle was an unusual child. For a start, there was her unusual name, though most people just called her BB. Then there was the fact that she didn't like sweet things. No chocolates, no lollipops, no sherbet or ice cream. Most unusual of all, Belinda Birtwistle loved mushrooms. What kind of kid likes mushrooms? Well, BB certainly did.

    She had her favorites, of course. Those round button mushrooms were just fine, and she quite liked the Chanterelles you would see occasionally at the market. The most delicious, in BB's eyes at least, was the wild Porcinis that her father would sometimes bring back from the forest. They were huge mushrooms that smelled like the leaves of the forest floor and which her mother would fry in butter before folding them gently into a giant omelet. That, in BB's opinion, was sheer heaven.

    BB couldn't always find mushrooms. Sometimes, she had to wait until just the right moment before they burst from the ground in the forest. They grew near old oak trees that only her father knew, and he would show no one his secret mushroom hunting places.

BB's dream was to be able to gather mushrooms for herself. When she learned to do that, she knew that she would be happy forever, but her father had strictly forbidden her to hunt mushrooms in the forest. It was, he told her, the most dangerous thing in the world if you gathered mushrooms when you didn't know what you were doing.

BB would beg her father to take her into the forest and teach her about mushrooms, but he always insisted that she was too small.

"You need to be patient," he would tell her. "When you are older, I will show the ways of the mushroom and even take you to some of my secret mushroom hunting places. But not until you are much older."

BB didn't want to wait until she was older. She wanted to hunt for mushrooms now. How difficult could it be, after all?

One day when her father was away working, BB decided that the time had come. She couldn't wait forever to learn about mushrooms. If her father didn't want to teach her, she would just have to teach herself. She collected a basket from the kitchen, and when her mother wasn't looking, she sneaked off into the woods.

It took over an hour before BB found her first mushroom. It was a big Porcini, although this one had a slightly bluish tinge to it that the ones her father found didn't have. That didn't matter. BB was sure that it would wash away or vanish when her mother cooked it. Soon after that, she found an even bigger one, and then, a few minutes later, she found three in a row. Her basket was almost full already, and BB decided that she would look for just one more before turning to head home. Already, she could imagine how pleased her mother would be when she arrived with a basket brimming with delicious mushrooms.

She was wandering with her head down, looking for that last mushroom of the day when suddenly she heard a voice.

"What do you have there in your basket, little girl?"

She jumped with fright, but when she turned around, she saw that the person talking to her was a little old man and she did not need to be afraid. He was tiny with a long grey beard and eyes that twinkled when he smiled.

"I am collecting mushrooms for my dinner," said BB proudly.

"Mmm," said the little old man. "May I have a look?"

BB showed him her basket, and as he looked inside, a frown crossed his face.

"You haven't collected mushrooms before, have you?" he asked.

BB was a little indignant. Who was he to doubt her abilities when she had been eating mushrooms for years and was so very fond of them?

"My father is always bringing me mushrooms, and I have been eating them for as long as I can remember."

"Eating them is one thing," he said. "Knowing which ones to collect is quite another. Do you know that there are mushrooms that are so poisonous that they can kill you?"

"These are Porcinis. My father often hunts them here, and my mother cooks them for me in butter."

The old man frowned again.

"I'm sorry young lady, but these are not Porcinis, though they look very similar. That is the trouble with mushrooms. There are some that are delicious and others that look very much like them that can make you very sick or even kill you."

BB was getting angry now. She was sure this little man was just saying that so he could steal her mushrooms and take them home for his own dinner.

"You don't believe me, do you? Here, let me prove it." He reached into his pocket and brought out a battered-looking pocketknife. "Have you watched your mother prepare the Porcinis when she was cooking them?"

"Of course," said **BB**. "In fact, I always help her because I love the smell when they are being fried."

The old man reached into her basket and lifted out one of her mushrooms.

"Do those mushrooms do this when you cut into them?" he asked, and with that, he cut her mushroom in half.

The flesh of the mushroom immediately turned blue, and even the blade of the knife changed color. **BB** couldn't believe her eyes.

"I've never seen that before," she said. She was sounding a little less sure of herself now.

"That's because these aren't Porcinis. I know that they look like they are, but they are deadly poisonous. If you had eaten these, you could have become very, very sick. In fact, when you get home, you should wash out the basket carefully and wash your hands well so that you don't accidentally rub the poison onto something else."

BB was still uncertain if this was some kind of trick. The old man was watching her with those sparkling eyes of his, and it was difficult to believe he was trying to steal her mushrooms. Even so, **BB** was not willing to give up such a delicious looking haul of mushrooms.

"You still don't believe me, do you?" he asked, smiling. "I'll tell you what. Why don't I walk you home, and then we can show your mushrooms to your dad? If he says they are all right to eat, they are all yours. If he says they are poison, then you will have to throw them away."

BB didn't like the idea, but she was too polite to say so, and so, with her new acquaintance, she headed for home. Her father was there when she arrived, and she could see he was angry that she had gone into the forest without telling anyone. She thought he might stop being angry when he saw her basket brimming with mushrooms, and so she ran up and showed him what she had found.

Her father took one look at what was in the basket, and then he told her she must wash her hands immediately while he threw the poison mushrooms away. After that, he sent her to bed with no dinner for disobeying him.

BB was so humiliated that she was crying as she climbed into bed. She could hear her father and the old man talking downstairs, but she couldn't hear what was being said. She had a pretty good idea they were saying what a stupid young girl she was.

She was still upset, but her eyelids were growing heavy, and she had nearly fallen asleep when she heard her father come into the room and sit down on the edge of her bed. She was convinced that she would get into more trouble but, instead, he took her hand and spoke gently to her.

"Belinda Birtwistle, you did a silly and dangerous thing today, but I know your intentions were good. Tomorrow I have arranged for you to go back into the woods with old Mr. Delaney, and he is going to teach you all about which mushrooms you can eat, and which ones are dangerous."

"Who is Mr. Delaney?"

"He is the old man who found you in the woods today. He is a wonderful old man, and nobody knows more about mushrooms than he does. In fact, it was he who taught me all about mushrooms when I wasn't much older than you are now."

BB was very excited, but she was tired too, and soon she fell fast asleep and dreamt of eating mushroom omelets.

Chapter 6: The Bear Who Was Too Big

Everyone knows that bears are big, but Benjamin was really big for a bear. Big though he was, Benjamin's best friends were bunnies. Most bears wandered the woods by themselves, doing little more than eating berries and scratching their backs on trees. The same could not be said for Benjamin.

Every afternoon, when the rabbits gathered in the grass and chased each other back and forth, Benjamin was there, playing and cavorting as though he was just another rabbit. The rabbits were so used to him they thought nothing of it. He was, in their eyes, just one of the gang.

Things became a little more complicated when Ralph, the rabbit, announced that it would soon be his birthday and that he would be having a party at his house. The whole gang was invited, and until then, it hadn't occurred to anyone that Benjamin couldn't come to Ralph's house. You see, rabbits live in holes in the ground, and there was no way you could fit a giant bear such as Benjamin down such a tiny hole.

Benjamin had really been excited about the party. He had never been to one before, and when he suddenly realized that he might not be able to go because he was so big, he became quite sad.

"I know," said Ralph. "We'll have the party outside on the grass. That way, Benjamin can come, and it won't matter that he is so big."

This idea seemed to please everyone, and especially Benjamin. In the days before the party, he became more and more excited until he was looking forward to it even more than Ralph was.

Finally, the big day came. All the rabbits and Benjamin gathered in the meadow outside Rogers's house. There, his mother had set up tables and chairs. The tables were covered in ice cream and jello, and there was a big carrot cake at one end with candles on the top. The weather was fine, and everything appeared to be perfect. That was until Benjamin sat down.

Bunny chairs aren't made for bears, and Benjamin's soon broke.

From there, things just went from bad to worse. When he breathed, he accidentally blew all the candles out that were on the cake. After that, and quite by mistake, he took a mouthful of jello and, in one gulp, finished enough jello for all the rabbits. He ate what he thought was a tiny slice of cake, but after that, there was little left for the others. The final straw came when he accidentally trod on one of Ralphs's presents and crushed it.

The big bear was so embarrassed that he went home and left the rabbits to play games by themselves. Benjamin decided that he shouldn't play with the rabbits anymore. He was, he realized, just too big a bear to be with bunnies.

Instead, he wandered in the woods by himself, where he became quite lonely. Though he missed his friends very much, he was so embarrassed by all that had gone wrong at Ralph's party; he didn't want to go back and make a fool of himself again. Instead, he ate berries and scratched his back on trees. On the days when the bunnies were playing in the grass, Benjamin would sometimes sneak down and watch them from the edge of the woods. How he missed the fun they used to have.

Weeks later, the bunnies were playing in the grass when a wolf spotted them. Wolves are very fond of bunnies. In fact, they regard them as one of their favorite foods. As soon as the wolf spotted all those little rabbits chasing one another through the grass, he got down on his belly and began to slowly creep toward them. Closer and closer, he crawled toward the unsuspecting little rabbits.

Soon he was just yards away, and he decided which bunny was the fattest and would make the best dinner. He licked his lips and then decided on a little girl rabbit named Esmerelda. He waited until the unsuspecting rabbit was quite close, and then the big gray wolf pounced. He was about to snatch Esmerelda up in his fierce jaws when suddenly there was a roar, and a giant bear came charging out of the woods toward him.

The startled rabbits bolted in all directions, and Esmeralda just avoided the wolves' flashing teeth. As his dinner escaped from his grasp at the last second, the wolf was furious, and he turned toward this audacious bear who had cost him his dinner.

Benjamin feared the ferocious wolf, but he had no choice now. A huge fight started, and the bear and the wolf went into battle. Fur flew, and teeth flashed. Claws and jaws slashed the air, and the rabbits watched in horror.

Finally, the fighting stopped, and the wolf limped back toward the woods. Cut and bleeding, Benjamin lay in the grass, and the rabbits ran toward him, fearing he might be dead.

Bears are strong, and although he needed to spend time in the hospital, Benjamin was soon on the mend. Every day, the bunnies would hop down to the hospital to visit their friend, the brave, bandaged bear. By the time he was well again, the bunnies had made him promise he would play with them again and told him they didn't mind at all that he was so big.

Chapter 7: The Prince Who Wasn't Brave

There are certain things that people expect of princes. They should always be honest, true, brave, and handsome. Okay—they might get away with being a little bit ugly sometimes, but honest, true, and brave are a must.

Prince Reginald Roger Regina was a wonderful prince. You couldn't want for a prince who was more honest and truer, and, if truth be told, he was a little on the handsome side too—in a cool, casual, kind of a way. The only thing that Reginald lacked was that he wasn't brave. He longed to be courageous and fearless, as a real prince should be, but he just wasn't.

Now, his people loved him anyway. He was so honest and true that it was difficult for them not to. But that didn't make Reginald feel any better. He knew that being brave was really important. The question was, how can you be brave when you aren't?

Reginald did everything in his power to be braver. He took advice from all the wisest men in the land and frequently talked with all of his bravest knights. They all had plenty of suggestions. Drink more milk, eat more spinach, and whistle in the dark were some of their many recommendations. Reginald tried them all—well, all except whistling in the dark. He was a little frightened of the dark. Things never seemed to improve.

All his knights and fellow courtiers would go jousting or hunting wild boar, Reginald preferred to stay at home and eat eggs on toast. He dreaded the day when his kingdom might go to war. He would be expected to lead his knights into battle, and Reginald could think of nothing worse.

His lack of courage was giving Reginald very little sleep. He would lie awake, trying to think brave thoughts or summon up courage, but the results were poor. When, eventually, he did get some sleep, he would often dream about fire breathing dragons, and he would wake up in a sweat with his heart pounding terribly.

One day, news arrived that the famous knight, Lancelot Livingstone, was coming to the castle on an official visit. Lancelot Livingstone was no ordinary knight. He was reputed to be the bravest knight in all the land and was said to have killed six dragons all by himself.

Reginald was desperate to ask him for advice on how to increase his courage, but even the thought of doing that made the young prince a little frightened. He sighed to himself. What a coward he felt he was.

Lancelot Livingstone was coming to the castle to visit Reginald's father, the king. A great banquet had been prepared in the knight's honor, and there were to be guests from across the kingdom.

When the big day arrived, Reginald hung back among the crowd and watched the famous knight from a distance. He was desperate to talk to him and discover what the secret was to the knight's extraordinary bravery, but with so many people around him all wanting to shake the knight's hand or have a quick selfie painted with him, it was impossible. Reginald knew that if he were a real and brave prince, he would just stride up to the knight and shake his hand warmly. The truth was, he was *too* afraid.

Sad and ashamed, Reginald slipped away from the crowd and found a quiet place in the castle grounds where he could sit down and be alone with his pain. Talking to Lancelot Livingstone had been his last hope of learning to be brave, and he didn't even have the courage to do that. Perhaps, he thought to himself, this was to be his destiny. Always too nervous about being the brave prince he so wanted to be.

As he sat there, feeling sorry for himself, he suddenly heard a sound behind him. He turned and who should be standing there but the famed knight, Lancelot Livingstone.

"Do you mind if I join you?" asked the knight. "I really hate being surrounded by so many people, and sometimes I just need to get away for a few minutes."

"Me too," said the young prince. He was dying to say more—to ask about being brave, but he wasn't sure that he could bring himself to do it.

"My name is Lancelot Livingstone," said the knight reaching out to shake hands.

"I'm Reginald," said the little prince. He didn't want to give his full name or tell the knight he was a prince because he was sure that Lancelot Livingstone would have heard about him and know what a coward he was.

"I guess you also don't like crowds?" said the knight.

"Not really," Reginald replied cautiously. This knight was so famous, and yet he seemed so ordinary.

"Me neither," said the knight as he sat down next to the young prince. "They make me a little nervous, actually."

"Crowds make you nervous? But I thought that you were the bravest knight in all of the lands and that you had fearlessly fought in hundreds of battles."

"Yes. But I was nervous before every single one of them," sighed the knight.

"How can that be? You are the bravest man in the land."

"Well, here's the thing," said Lancelot Livingstone. "A man can be scared. That's perfectly normal. It is a matter of doing what you have to do even though you are scared. That is what counts."

"So, you are telling me that you were scared before every battle?" asked Reginald in amazement.

"Absolutely. Sometimes I was shaking so badly that I thought I was going to fall off my horse."

"But then why do people say you are so brave?" Reginald wanted to know.

"Because even though I was scared, I went into battle anyway."

Reginald thought about this for a moment. Suddenly, being scared didn't seem so important anymore. Maybe he wasn't the terrible boy he thought he was.

"I'm often scared," he admitted to the knight.

"I think most people are scared a lot of the time. Some of them are just better at pretending they aren't than others are. I don't think pretending to be brave is the same thing as actually being brave. Brave is when you do something even though you are scared."

Reginald realized that he could do this. He could do things even though she was scared. From that moment on, he decided that when he was scared, he would do things anyway. He would stop thinking about his fear and would just focus on what had to be done. Once he had made that momentous decision, he was soon sleeping soundly again.

He became friends with Lancelot Livingstone, and eventually, he became king. The people would think of him as one of the bravest kings they had ever had. And he was honest and true—and just a little bit handsome.

Chapter 8: The Dragon Whisperer

Many, many years ago, dragons roamed the earth and lived alongside people. Some dragons were quite harmless, others were a nuisance, and some were dangerous. What you have to understand is there were different kinds of dragons. There were the small ones who were not much different from large lizards, the water ones who lived mainly in the sea, and sometimes in large lakes, and there were the huge ones who breathed fire when they chose to.

It was the really big ones who normally caused most problems. They were mainly omnivorous, which meant that they ate everything. If they ate the farmer's cows and sheep, that would become a big problem. If they ate people, that would be a bigger problem still.

If you lived in a village or a town where a dragon became a problem, then there were people you could call on who would come and deal with the dragon. They were a bit like the pest control people we call today if you get mice in your house, except they rode horses and carried swords. Many of these warriors who dealt with bad dragons were knights. They would ride around the countryside, and when they heard that a village was having a dragon problem, they would ride to that town and agree on a fee for getting rid of the dragon. It was dangerous work, and so the dragon fighters would charge a lot of money. If you were living in a small village, there was a good chance that you were poor, but you still had to find the money because it was too dangerous to have a bad dragon around.

Such was the case in the village of Lugobrick in the high Dochnia Mountains. The village was small and very poor. They mainly kept cows and goats, and they made what little money they earned from making cheese. One day, a big dragon moved into a cave just above the village. No one knows why he lived there, but he did.

The first that the village knew about the matter was when they woke up one morning to find that two of their goats were missing. At first, the people thought that the goats might have been taken by wolves, but when they investigated, they saw the unmistakable tracks of a large dragon. Dragons have very long claws, so their tracks are easy to identify. They also leave a mark on the earth as they drag their giant tails along behind them.

The people hoped that the dragon was just passing through and that he might soon go away. They hid in their houses, but two days later, the dragon struck again. This time, he ate one of the farmer's cows. Now the farmers from the village were getting desperate. They couldn't afford to keep losing their animals. They sent word out to the neighboring villages they needed a dragon slayer, and the word soon spread from village to village, that Lugobrick had a dragon problem.

A few days later, a knight came riding up to the village. He looked very impressive to the poor farmers. He rode a big black stallion and had on a shining suit of armor. Behind him ran a young boy whose job it was to carry the knight's shield and sword when he didn't need them. The knight met with the elders of the village and agreed to kill the dragon for twenty pieces of gold and three cows. That was a lot of money, and the whole village would have to hand over all of their savings, but what choice did they have? If the dragon stayed, he might eat all of their cows and goats, and then what would they do to make a living. Also, maybe the dragon might become hungry, and he might then start eating them.

At first light the following morning, the knight mounted his horse, drew his sword, and rode up toward the cave where the dragon was now living. Two hours later, he was back. His hair was all singed, and he had lost his sword. The dragon was too strong for him, and he could not deal with it. He left the village in shame.

Now the farmers were even more worried. The dragon was still in the cave, and they didn't know what to do. If the knight couldn't deal with it, they certainly couldn't. The next morning another knight rode into the village. He was riding a big white stallion that was even more impressive than the one the last knight had been riding. He, too, had heard about the dragon and he was convinced he could get rid of it. The only problem was, he was even more expensive than the previous knight. He demanded twenty pieces of gold and five cows to free the people from the terrible dragon. Once again, the people had to agree. They simply didn't have a choice.

That very afternoon, the knight rode his big white stallion out of the village and into the hills where the dragon's cave was. He was back again just before nightfall, and he was in terrible shape. He was covered in smoke and soot and had lost both his helmet and his shield. The dragon had won again, and now the people had no idea what to do.

The dragon hunting knights stopped coming after that. Word had got around that the dragon at Lugobrick was just too dangerous, and the knights didn't want to fight it. In the village, things were getting desperate. Every morning, when the farmers went out into the fields, they would find that one or two of their animals were missing. Things were getting so desperate that some villagers were talking of moving away.

It was uncertain how long this state of affairs could continue, but one morning the villagers woke up to see a man riding towards the village on a donkey. They didn't know who he was, but it was clear that he wasn't a dragon-slaying knight. When he reached the villagers, he told them he was there to sort out their dragon problem. His appearance was so unimpressive that some villagers laughed at him.

The villagers had nothing to lose, so they asked how much this new contender wanted for freeing them of the dragon.

"I would like three wheels of cheese," said the young man confidently. "Oh, and I would also like to marry the prettiest maiden in the village."

Nobody from Lugobrick believed this young man could do what he claimed. He didn't even possess a sword or a shield, and his mount was an old donkey. With nothing to lose, they agreed to his terms and then gathered in the village square to watch as he rode out to engage with the dragon. It was late afternoon by then, and neither the young man nor the donkey returned that night. The villagers all feared that the foolish young man and his donkey had been eaten by the dragon.

The next morning, however, the man rode back into town, looking totally unharmed and relaxed.

"I have come to collect my three wheels of cheese and your most beautiful maiden," he told the surprised-looking villagers.

"But what about the dragon?" they asked. "How have you dealt with him?"

"Oh, he is sleeping up in his cave. He won't wake up again for at least one hundred years."

The villagers eyed him suspiciously.

"How do we know you are not lying and trying to trick us?" they asked.

"Well, that is easy," he replied with a smile. "You can send someone up to the cave, and there you will see the dragon lying fast asleep."

The villagers were now sure this was a trick, so several sneaked up to the cave where the dragon had taken up residence. Sure enough, they could see the dragon curled up and sleeping on the cave floor. Nervously they threw a stone at it to see if it would wake up, but nothing happened. They then poked it with a long stick, and still, the beast did not stir. Eventually, some even walked up to it and shouted in its ear, but the dragon just kept right on sleeping.

When they returned to the village to tell the others what they had seen, the people were amazed.

"But how did you do that?" they all asked.

"I just sat down with him and whispered bedtime stories," replied the young man. "Surely everyone knows that dragons can't resist a good bedtime story!"

Some people believed him, but some still remained suspicious.

"How can we be sure that if we pay you that, the dragon won't wake up as soon as you are gone and start his mischief again?"

The young man thought about this for a while.

"I'll tell you what," he suggested. "Let me have my cheese and let me marry your fairest maiden, and I will stay in the village for five years. If the dragon doesn't strike again in that time, my wife and I will be free to go on our way."

The villagers discussed this idea, deciding they would give the couple a wedding feast and loaned them a house and land where they could stay. In fact, they were so happy with this wonderful man who could farm while he was there. After five years, they had become so settled that the couple didn't leave, and instead, they stayed on in Lugobrick, making it their forever home.

The dragon is still sleeping in the cave above the town, and now and then, the young man saddles his donkey and rides off for a few days to whisper stories to other troublesome dragons in the nearby villages. He has become quite famous, but it hasn't changed him. He still lives in the village, and every night he whispers fairytales to his two small children, and they fall fast asleep.

Chapter 9: A Tale of The Broken Tail

Most people probably don't realize that the main way that mermaids get around is by using their tail. That is how they glide through the water with such grace and speed. To a mermaid, a tail is as important as legs are to humans.

I will now tell you a story about a young mermaid named Cindy. Cindy was a very happy young mermaid, much like any other. She loved playing with her friends and exploring the beautiful underwater world in which she spent most of her life. It was filled with colorful fish, bright coral, and dark and frightening caves. In short, it was the most wonderful place to investigate and play. Mermaids didn't really go to school as human children did. Instead, they learned from exploring the world around them.

Life was good beneath the ocean, and there were really only two things that mermaids had to fear. One was big sharks, and the other was humans. Mermaids learned from a very early age that sharks liked to eat them and so they were always on the lookout for these big gray enemies.

Humans were a slightly different matter. Most mermaids had heard stories about how dangerous humans could be, but none had ever met anyone who had contacted a human. Humans lived on land and mainly ventured out to sea in boats, so they inhabited a very different world to that of the mermaids. Unlike sharks, which they knew were dangerous, humans were a mystery to mermaids, and so they were very curious about them. They loved to spy on them from a distance and would laugh among themselves about the human's funny looking legs and the fact that they couldn't even breathe underwater.

As time went on and the humans came to sea in boats with big smelly motors, there were more of them around. This meant that on the one hand, there were more of them to spy on, but on the other, there was more chance of them being seen by these land-dwelling people.

One day, when Cindy and her friends were so busy playing they let their guard down, a big shark snuck up on them. Normally mermaids are very vigilant, but they had been having such fun they simply didn't pay attention. Suddenly one of Cindy's friends caught sight of the shark and called out a warning. In a flash, all the mermaids fled for cover, but Cindy was a little slower than the others, and the shark was almost on top of her before she knew it. She just managed to duck out of the way of his jagged jaws and slip into a cave, but she could sense he was not far behind her.

The caves were frightening places, but having the shark right behind her was even more frightening. Cindy had little choice but to swim deeper into the dark passages, hoping to lose the hungry shark. Suddenly she saw a narrow tunnel through the rock, and she ducked into it, hoping that it would be too tight a fit for the shark. The tunnel grew narrower and narrower, and she was sure the shark wouldn't be able to squeeze through, but she was too scared to even look over her shoulder.

She felt a powerful tug on her tail that brought her to a dramatic stop, and she was convinced the shark had got her. In fact, the shark had given up chasing her as soon as she had swum into the tunnel, but Cindy didn't know that. Instead, she had kept on swimming at a dangerous speed, and now her tail had become caught between the narrow walls of the tunnel. Cindy was trapped, and her tail was badly damaged, but at least she had managed to lose the shark.

It was hours before she freed herself, and even then, it was only because she had help from her friends. They had wanted to come earlier, but the hungry shark had hung around for ages, hoping to catch the little mermaid as she came back out of the cave. Her friends gathered around her and helped her make her way home.

Over time, the tail healed, and the pain stopped, but Cindy would never be the fast swimmer she had been before the shark chased her. That meant that she had to be very careful, and if a shark ever chased her again, she was in great danger. Even just playing with her friends was not as much fun now because she was so much slower than they were, and she couldn't always join in. They were kind and waited for her, of course. Mermaids are always kind, but it just wasn't the same.

One afternoon, Cindy and her friends were hanging out on the surface of the water spying on the humans. It was something they often did with Cindy because it was a game that didn't require too much speed or put too much strain on her injury. They were watching a sleek new motorboat as it cruised slowly through the water. There were several humans on deck, and they appeared to look for something.

Suddenly one human swung his binoculars around in their direction, and he must have seen them because he pointed in their direction, and the boat turned. Her friends were so fast they disappeared from sight very quickly, but as usual, Cindy was slow. The boat moved quickly in her direction, and she simply wasn't fast enough to get away.

She was swimming as fast as she could, and still, the boat was gaining on her. The humans were all hanging over the edge of the boat and pointing in her direction. Cindy tried to go a little bit faster, but her tail hurt, and she slowed down even more.

Eventually, the boat drew up alongside her, and one human threw a net over her. Now there was no chance of getting away. The net tangled her up, and soon she felt herself being pulled from the water. She was terrified and had no idea what to do. She could hear the people shouting at one another.

"Is that the one?" one of them yelled as they lifted her onto the deck of the boat.

"Yes, definitely. You can see by the way she was swimming that she is the one we saw last week. She has an injury on her tail," somebody answered.

"Be careful with her!" another person shouted. "We don't want to hurt her."

"Look how beautiful she is," a different voice called out – one of the women.

"Quickly. Get out of the way so the vet can get through. He must treat her and get her back in the water as soon as possible."

By then, the net had been removed, and Cindy was lying on the deck, looking up at a circle of people peering down at her. She was so frightened that all she could do was cry.

A lady carrying a big black bag pushed through the crowd and kneeled down by her tail. Cindy could feel her touching it. It wasn't sore, but with all the people around and the tears in her eyes, she had no idea what the lady was doing.

"It doesn't look too bad," said the lady they were calling the vet. "I have given her some injections, and I think that should heal her. We need to get her back in the water."

Minutes later, Cindy was being lowered back into the sea, and all the humans were lined up along the edge of the boat watching her. Some waved, but Cindy was too shocked and frightened to wave back.

Instead, she turned and slowly swam away from the boat and the strange humans on board.

It was several days before Cindy got over her shock. When she did, the first thing she noticed was that her tail no longer hurt when she used it. Within days she was able to swim normally again, and soon she was as fast and agile as she had ever been.

It took a long time, and lots of thought before Cindy realized that the kind humans had somehow healed her and freed her from her pain. It was strange to realize that creatures she had feared all her life could actually turn out to be kind. After that, she would often swim out to that spot in the ocean where they had caught her in their net. When she saw the boat, she would wave and smile, and, if they saw her, they would always wave and smile back.

Cindy wished that she could thank them for the great kindness they had bestowed on her, but the mermaid knew it would never be. The world of humans and mermaids must remain forever separate, except for very rare occasions. Cindy was just glad she had enjoyed one special event.

Chapter 10: The Mean Twin

Many years ago, there were two princesses who were identical twins, looking so much alike that even their own parents sometimes had trouble telling them apart. That was where their similarities ended, however. In character, these sisters differed greatly from one another.

The eldest, by a minute or two, was named Anabella, and her younger sister was called Anastasia. Anabella was very self-important, and she spent a great deal of time looking at herself in the mirror and trying on clothes. Anastasia liked to spend time with other people and would often help the maids with their chores in the kitchen. This would annoy Anabella immensely.

"We are royal princesses," she would say in frustration. "It is beneath us to be seen working with the servants."

"I don't see any reason why being kind is something that princesses should not do." the younger sister would respond.

This would make Anabella even angrier. She didn't believe in kindness. She only believed in being beautiful and powerful. She was so nasty that many courtiers feared for the kingdom if she should one day become queen. She seemed to take pleasure in ordering people about, but because she was a royal princess and next in line to the throne, there was nothing that anyone could do.

One day Anabella went for a walk in the forest that surrounded the castle. It was not something she often did. The forest was dirty and damp, and there were no mirrors in which she could look at her reflection. She had only went for a walk because Anastasia was helping some maids with tidying in the castle, and the whole idea made her so angry that she just had to get away.

As she wandered through the woods, her anger toward her sister grew, and she became bitter and angry. She was thinking angry thoughts when she stumbled on a tiny pond in a bright glade of sunshine. It was surrounded by beautiful plants, and damselflies and dragonflies darted across the surface of the water. On the far side of the pond, a gorgeous kingfisher sat peering into the pond hoping to catch a small fish.

Anabella saw none of this beauty. All she saw was a chance of seeing her own beauty reflected on the water. As for the princess, the pond was nothing more than a giant mirror in which she could admire herself. She moved closer to the pond, and when she reached the water's edge, she knelt down to get a better look at her reflection.

At first, all she could see was a bitter young girl with thin angry lips, but gradually her composure returned, and as she controlled her anger, she could see her beauty again. Suddenly, just as she was enjoying looking at herself again, the image she saw reflected was shattered as the kingfisher dived into the water like an arrow. He appeared again seconds late with a silverfish flapping in his beak. Anabella was furious again. She picked up a small stone and threw it at the startled bird and shouted at it to make it go away.

"That wasn't very kind," said a voice behind her that made the princess jump.

Anabella turned around to see a withered and bent old lady dressed in rags standing just behind her. She didn't have time to wonder how the old hag had gotten so close without her hearing.

"I don't have to be kind," she snapped. "I am a princess and heir to the royal throne."

"I know very well who you are, young lady. You are the one the people refer to as the princess without a heart."

"And what would you know?" demanded Anabella.

"Oh," said the old lady, "I know a great many things; things that you will never learn because you are too busy admiring yourself in the mirror. Look at all this beauty that you are surrounded by, and yet you fail to see any of it."

Anabella was beside herself with rage. Who was this mere peasant who would dare to talk to a royal princess this way?

"How dare you!" she snapped. "Don't you know that I could have you thrown into the dungeons with just a word?"

The old woman didn't even look slightly afraid at Anabella's outburst.

"Young lady, if you knew who I was and how much power I have, it would be you that would be afraid. I am going to give you one chance. Give me a coin to buy myself some bread and cheese, and I will ignore your petulant anger."

That was just too much for Anabella. Who was this foolish old hag who would dare defy a princess and then on top of it demand money from her?

"Give me your name, old woman. This very day I will see to it that you are dragged away in chains and thrown into the castle dungeons where it is cold and dark. There you will eat bread, but I doubt very much that you will ever taste cheese again."

"My name is Zelda, though the people around here call me the wise one. As for me going down to the royal dungeons, I don't think so. In fact, things are about to get very bad for you." With that, Zelda clicked her fingers, and the once beautiful princess was suddenly transformed into a toad.

When the princess did not return to the castle by nightfall, everyone became very concerned about her, and search parties were sent out, but they could find no sign of the princess. For weeks, the palace staff and people from the nearby villages continued to search for Anabella, but she was nowhere to be found. In the end, the searches were called off, and it was believed that the princess must have either run away or been kidnapped.

Though Anastasia and her twin sister were very different, and though they had never gotten along, Anastasia missed Anabella very much. That her sister was missing meant that it was likely that she would one day inherit the throne, but Anastasia didn't care about that. She didn't want to become queen. All she wanted was to see her sister again.

One day, long after most people had given up hope and when all the search parties had been called off, Anastasia went down to the forest where she always loved to wander. She made her way to the lake where she had fond memories of the wonderful flowers and of sitting quietly, admiring the beauty and watching the kingfisher hunt for little fish.

As she sat down and dangled her feet in the water, she suddenly saw a big toad. It was not unusual for her to see toads and frogs so near to the water, but this one seemed unusual. Instead of keeping still in the hope of not being seen or simply hopping away, this one was hopping toward her as though trying to attract her attention. In fact, Anastasia noted, it was an exceptionally brave toad. Not only did it not flee or hide, but it also hopped right up onto her knee and looked her in the eye as though trying to say something.

Anastasia was not the least bit afraid. Instead, she was curious. Why would a toad behave in such a strange manner? She tried placing it back on the grass in case it was just confused, but the toad hopped right back up onto her knee. That was peculiar. Eventually, the young princess was no longer sure what she should do, and so she put the peculiar toad in her pocket and take it home with her.

Perhaps, she thought to herself, it would be happier if she released it near one of the many ponds on the grounds of the palace.

As she was making her way back along the path towards the palace, she came across an old hag standing there watching her carefully. It was the same old woman who had turned her sister into a toad, but Anastasia had no idea about that.

"Do you have a coin for an old lady?" she asked. "I haven't eaten for three whole days."

Anastasia dug in her pockets and came up with a small silver coin, which she handed the old woman with a smile.

"If you like," the princess said, "I could take you back to the palace and ask the cook to prepare you something."

"You are very kind," said the old woman with a sly smile. "And in return for your kindness, I would like to grant you one wish. Ask me for anything, and I will give it to you."

Anastasia was a bit taken aback. How could this poor old woman possibly offer her anything when she was a rich princess, and the old woman was little more than a poor beggar-woman?

"I only have one thing that I want," she answered, "and I doubt that you could give it to me. I would be to have my sister back with me."

"Ah," said the old woman with a smile. "You are talking about young Princess Anabella."

"Yes, that's right. How did you know about her?"

"I know many things, my dear. You have shown me great kindness, and now you will have your reward. When you get back to the palace, remove that ugly toad you have hidden in your pocket, and you will get your sister back. Perhaps she will have learned a lesson from the kindness you have shown me."

Anastasia was still confused, but she rushed back toward the palace. How could this woman possibly know about her sister, and how could she have known of the toad she had hidden in her pocket and which she had been careful not to let her see?

As soon as she got into the palace gardens, she reached for the toad, but to Anastasia's surprise, it was no longer there. She turned to look for it, but there, in front of her, stood Anabella. The two sisters jumped into one another's arms, and soon the whole palace was celebrating.

The king and queen held a huge ball, inviting all of those people who had helped to search for their daughter. To their great surprise, however, Anabella said she didn't want a ball in her honor. Instead, she asked that her mother and father take the money and use it to feed the poor people from the surrounding villages.

Anabella was a changed person after that. She became far less interested in how she looked and began to think about helping those who were less fortunate than herself. The people were suspicious at first but, over time, she won them over and she became almost as popular with them as Princess Anastasia had always been.

Chapter 11: The Three Naughty Brothers

In a small village called Kokcho, there lived three brothers. They were widely known as the naughtiest boys in town, and they were regularly in trouble. They came from a very rich family, but their father was often away on business, and because he was seldom around, there was nobody to discipline them. To be fair, their mother did try, but the boys were just too much for her. It became far easier for her to just give them money and send them to town than it was for her to manage their mischief.

Saturday mornings were the time when you were most likely to find them playing in the village streets and looking for trouble. Another boy from the village was called Pieter, and he knew the three brothers well because he was at the same school as them. Actually, because Kokcho was such a small village, all the children from the town were at the same school as he was.

Although all three brothers were older than Pieter, one of them was in his class, and two were in class a year behind him. This was because the boys were so naughty and never did their homework, so they had all been held back a class or two. Pieter's family was far from rich, like the brothers' family was. His father was a poor shoemaker, and there was seldom any spare cash for them to enjoy. However, they were a happy family, and though Pieter was an only child, his parents were very proud of him and tried hard to give him little presents from time to time.

One Saturday morning, Pieter's father took him aside and gave him a few pennies and told his son to go to town and buy himself candy. This was a big treat for Pieter, and as he walked to town, he allowed his mind to wander and dream of the sweet delights he would buy for himself. He couldn't decide between caramel creams and marshmallow balls, but he wanted chocolate coated raisins and a raspberry stick.

There was only one store in Kokcho that sold sweets. It was a general dealer, and it also sold milk, bread, cheese and vegetables, but it was the candy that most attracted Pieter. The store was owned by an old man called Mr. Krevit. He was wrinkled and bent, but he had eyes that sparkled and a delightful smile that showed the gaps where his teeth had once been. Running the store had made Mr. Krevit quite rich, and he drove a big black car - probably the most expensive car in town.

When Pieter entered the store, he saw the shelves of candy that ran down the middle of the store. It was heaving with different sweet delicacies, and Pieter's noticed it right away. He put his hand into his pocket to make sure that his pennies were still there, and then he wandered along the shelves, adding and subtracting as he did, so he could get the most for his money.

As he turned around the end of the row to start up the next one, he spotted the three brothers, and one of them was just slipping some candy into his pocket. Mr. Krevit was talking on the phone behind his counter, and he wouldn't have noticed what was happening.

As soon as the brothers saw that Pieter had noticed that they were stealing, they put their fingers on their lips and signaled that Pieter should keep quiet.

"You better not say anything," the oldest brother whispered to Pieter threateningly. "Here, take some yourself, and we can all leave with a few candies from old man Krevit."

"No way," said Pieter looking shocked. "I am not a thief, and you shouldn't be either."

"It's not really stealing," whispered one of the other brothers. "Mr. Krevit will never notice. Look how much candy there is here."

"That's not the point," said Pieter. "If it's not stealing, then what is it then? Do you think that if you take something small now that in years to come, you won't start stealing bigger things?"

By then, the brothers were getting quite angry that Pieter would not go along with their plans.

"Well, you don't have to take any if you don't want to, but you better not tell Krevit, or you will be in big trouble."

"Yeah," joined another brother. "We don't like snitches around here."

"Well, it just so happens that I don't like thieves," said Pieter.

In the heat of the argument, none of the boys had noticed that Mr. Krevit had finished on the phone and quietly made his way up behind them. He had heard nearly all arguments that had been taking place. He reached out one of his old arms and grabbed the oldest of the three brothers by the ear.

"I think we all need to have a little chat," he said, leading his victim toward the counter. He made all three brothers empty their pockets, and the haul he discovered was impressive. There were packets of sherbet, peppermint humbugs, licorice laces, and several bars of chocolate.

"Well," said the old man. "Who is going to pay for all this?"

The brothers looked at one another.

"Perhaps I will have to call Constable Watts? He might have something to say about this."

The brothers were all looking nervous. Suddenly they weren't the tough guys they had been just a few minutes before when they were threatening Pieter. Two begged Mr. Krevit not to call the constable, while the youngest brother simply burst into tears.

Mr. Krevit thought for a few minutes.

"I'll tell you what I am going to do," he said quietly. "First of all, I am going to give you three a bucket and sponge, and you are going to spend the rest of the morning washing my car. Secondly, you are banned from my store, and you will have to agree never to come in here again because I am sure that this is not the first time that this has happened. Do we have a deal?"

The boys had little choice, but they were happy to do anything that Mr. Krevit asked if he didn't call the village constable. He sent the boys off with a bucket to wash his car, which was parked in the hot sun. By then, Pieter had chosen his sweets and carefully added his pennies to make sure that he could pay for everything he had picked. He carried his haul over to the counter and laid it down next to the pile of candy that the brothers had tried to steal.

Mr. Krevit looked at Pieter's pile and at his pennies, and then he shook his head.

"Pieter, that was very brave of you." He then piled all the candy that Pieter had chosen and placed it in a paper bag along with what the brothers had stolen. "That is the reward for your honesty," he said, refusing to take the money that the young boy was holding out.

Pieter left the shop with the biggest haul of candy he had ever had. As he headed home, he could see the three brothers sweating in the heat of the sun as they washed Mr. Krevit's car.

"Make sure it shines so that I can see the reflection of my face in the paintwork," he heard that old man shouting to them as he headed up the street.

Chapter 12: Dragon Ball

There is something about dragons that many of us humans miss. You see, dragons are not all the same. There are many types of dragons.

There are dragons with wings that fly really high.

Fire-breathing dragons who light up the sky.

Dragons with tails.

Dragons with claws.

Sharp, pointed ears.

Or big hungry jaws.

There are some types of the dragon as big as a house.

And others somewhere between a cat and a mouse.

Many dragons that wander the world are friendly and can't even breathe fire. They live on only berries, leaves, and the occasional peach if they can find one. Most dragons are quite shy, which is why we rarely see them. They live in dark caves and deep valleys. Most of them wouldn't dream of harming anyone, and they certainly wouldn't want to be seen on television or in a movie like dragons you often see these days.

One thing that most dragons love is to play a game called dragon ball. This is a lot like football, except that you also may hit the ball with your tail. In the mountains of Gadoma was a flat field that was once very popular with many of the local dragon kids as a dragon ball field. All the types of dragon would gather there on Saturday afternoon when they would divide themselves into two teams and spend the next few hours playing DB (as they liked to refer to dragon ball).

On this particular occasion, all the dragons had gathered together for the usual Saturday afternoon of sport—all that is, except for the two brothers Rastafire and Lykaburn. This pair seldom joined in with the other dragons because they hated to lose and because they preferred to wander into the forest and work on their fire breathing techniques. They weren't supposed to do this, but they did it anyway.

The rest of the dragons gathered together, and soon the game was in full swing. Many of the smaller dragons were not as fast as the big dragons, but they were a kind bunch and so they were always encouraged to join in. As the game was progressing, one team captain, Lekie, stopped and sniffed the wind.

"I can smell smoke," he said.

Just then, the ball whizzed past him toward the goal, and he was forced to chase after it to prevent a goal being scored. A few minutes later, he stopped again to sniff the air. This time the others stopped too because the smell of smoke was becoming quite strong.

"What do you think it is?" asked Piwi. Piwi was a tiny little dragon who was so slow that he was terrible at dragon ball, but he was very popular with the other kids, none the less. Although he was slow, they always let him play, and his determination made up for his lack of speed.

"I think that Rastafire and Lykaburn have set the forest on fire," answered Lekie. Even as he was speaking, they saw the first thin wisps of smoke appearing above the trees further up the hill.

"Perhaps we should go down toward the river, just in case," said one of the other dragons.

"No, let's play DB a little bit longer. It's probably nothing," said another dragon.

Those dragons really loved to play dragon ball, so soon they were tearing around after the ball again, and for a few moments, any thoughts of fire were forgotten. That all changed when Piwi spoke again.

"I can see flames," he wailed.

The dragons stopped their game again, and by then, it was clear that Piwi was right. Bright orange flames were visible among the trees.

"Okay. Everyone to the river," said Lekie.

There was a strong wind that day, and the river was still some distance away. By the time they reached the riverbanks, the smoke was getting thick, and it was clear they were in danger.

"Swim to the other side," ordered Lekie, who remained as calm as he always did. Some dragons don't like water, but none had a choice, and so they all swam across the river where the fire wouldn't be able to reach them. Those that were strong swimmers helped those who were not so comfortable in the water.

When they were safely on the other side, Lekie did a headcount, and it was soon clear that one dragon was missing.

"Where's Piwi?" he asked in concern. The other dragons all looked at each other.

"We haven't seen him since we left the field," one dragon said. "You know how slow he is."

Lekie looked across the river where the smoke was making things almost dark, and it was easy to see flames jumping from tree to tree.

"You all stay here," yelled Lekie. "I'm going back for Piwi."

"You can't do that!" the others yelled. "It's too dangerous."

Before anyone could stop him, Lekie had dived back into the water and was swimming to the other side. When he climbed out, the smoke was so thick it was difficult to breathe, and he could hardly see where he was going. Bravely he pushed ahead anyway, though it was so hot that he had to cover his face with his arm. He moved up the hill toward the DB field, but the situation was desperate.

Choking from the smoke and battling the heat, Lekie pushed forward, but he knew he would never make it all the way to the field. He was just about to give up when he heard a small croaky voice coming from somewhere in the blackness.

"Help me!"

"Piwi, where are you?"

Lekie drove himself forward, though he was feeling his way rather than seeing anything. Eventually, he was so hot that he was about to give up when his hand suddenly fell on a tiny tail. Grabbing it, he tugged, and soon he had the little dragon tucked under his arm.

He turned and ran down the hill as fast as his dragon legs would carry him, but by now, the flames were gaining speed, and for a moment, it looked as though he wouldn't make it back to the river. For an instant, the smoke cleared slightly, and Lekie saw the light bouncing off the water's surface. At least he was running in the right direction, he thought to himself. He ran forward as fast as he could, and then, as soon as he was close enough, he dived into the water with Piwi still tucked under his arm.

The other dragons saw them coming and swam out to help them make it back to safety. When they got across the river, the two dragons lay on the shore, too weak to move but safe at last. The tip of Lekie's tail was burned, and most of Piwi's scales had been singed, but other than that, the pair were unharmed.

Soon after that, they heard the siren of the one tired old fire engine from the village of Gadoma. The village was poor and could afford only one fire engine, but the firemen were soon fighting the fire bravely, and eventually, they got the blaze under control; only after that was it safe for the dragon kids to come back across the river.

That night, as he lay in bed with his mother sat next to him, Lekie tried to tell her all about the adventure he had been through. His eyelids were heavy, and he kept nodding off halfway through the story. His bed was warm and inviting and, in the end, he knew that his need for sleep was stronger than he was.

Days later, Lekie was given an award for his bravery by the mayor. His biggest reward, though, was having his friend Piwi back with him safe and sound. Rastafire and Lykaburn never did own up to starting that fire, and to this day, nobody is really sure if they were responsible or not. But, thankfully, everyone is safe.

Chapter 13: The Fish That Danced

Lokie, the dragon, and some of his friends were very fond of fishing. They loved nothing better than to gather their fishing gear and head for the small river that flowed past the edge of the town. There, they would cast their hooks into the river and catch whatever fish they could.

On one particular day, Lokie and his friends Archie and Gerald made their way to the river, and in the space of just two hours, they had caught over ten fish. They were congratulating themselves on what a wonderful success they had had when Lokie noticed that it was getting late.

"We'll each have one more cast, and then we better get going," he said. "If we are late getting home, then we'll be in big trouble even if we do come home with lots of fish for dinner."

Gerald had the first cast, but he didn't even get a bite. Beside him, Archie had a bite, but whatever it was that had snatched his bait soon got away, which only left Lokie with his line in the water. He was just about to give up when his line suddenly went tight, and the tip of his fishing rod bent.

He pulled and strained, but whatever was on the other end of the line was not giving up without a fight. At one stage, it looked as though the rod might break, but Lokie fought the fish without breaking the rod or his line. The struggle continued for over half an hour before finally, with some help from his two friends, they dragged the fish from the water. It was the biggest fish any of them had ever caught, and as it lay on the grass, they looked at it in amazement. It wasn't like any fish the three young dragons had ever seen before. It had big gold scales that looked a bit like gold coins and very large eyes.

"Wow," exclaimed Archie. "I've never seen such a big fish. Who would imagine such a creature could come out of our little river?"

"Your family will be eating fish for a week," said Gerald.

Just then, a very surprising thing happened. The fish spoke.

"If you will return me to the water and let me go, I will grant you three wishes," it said.

"What do you think?" asked Lokie looking at his friends.

"I think it's your fish, so you should be the one to decide." said Archie to Lokie.

"Okay, Mr. Fish," said Lokie. "My friend Archie needs new soccer shoes, and so does my friend Gerald."

"That would make two wishes," the fish pointed out quickly.

"That doesn't matter," replied Lokie. "They both really need those shoes."

"Fine," said the fish, and he stood up on his tail and gave a slight bow toward the three little dragons. There was a loud explosion and a flash of light, and the air was filled with smoke. As the smoke cleared and the dragons saw again, it became clear that both Gerald and Archie were now wearing brand new soccer shoes.

"That's amazing," yelled Archie. "What are you going to ask for next?"

"You could use some new shoes yourself," suggested Gerald.

Lokie was quiet for a few moments, but then he finally spoke.

"I think for my last wish, I would like a new fire engine for the village. The one we have is really old, and it would be nice if we could have a new one."

The fish, who was still standing on his tail, gave a quick little dance followed by one of his silly looking bows, and once again, there was a loud explosion, and the air became filled with smoke. This time when the smoke cleared, a bright red fire engine stand on the grass beside the three dragons.

"Well, Mr. Fish, you have certainly honored your word, and so now it is time for us to honor ours. You are free to go."

"You were very generous about making wishes for others," said the fish," and because you thought of others before yourself, I am going to grant you one further wish, as an exceptional circumstance, you understand."

"Well, that is a surprise," said Lokie. "I think I would like a new scarf for my mother. Hers is getting really old, and she is in need of a new one."

With a twirl and a twist, followed by another little bow by the fish, there was another explosive sound and another cloud of smoke. When the smoke cleared, a beautiful silk scarf lie on the grass.

"And with that," said the fish, "it is time that I left you. He gave another twirl and a twist, followed by a neat little backflip, and he disappeared into the water. By then, the dragons were really late, but everyone forgave them when they rode into town and presented the fire chief with a brand-new fire engine.

Later that night, as he lay in bed, his mother came to say good night. She was wearing her new scarf, and she sat beside Lokie as he told her once more about the fish that danced. He had told the story often since their return, but now it was late, and it had been an exciting day. Halfway through the story, his eyes started to close, and he didn't make it to the end this time before he fell asleep. Once she was sure that he was sleeping deeply, his mother crept out of the room and returned a few minutes later carrying new soccer shoes for Lokie. He would find them when he woke up in the morning. That was his mother's reward to Lokie for thinking of others before himself.

Chapter 14: The Poor Boy and The Dragon

In a land far away, there once lived a very poor boy. He shared a small hut with his grandmother and his baby sister. His parents had long ago died, and his grandmother had agreed to take on the two orphans. When you're old, looking after two small children can be very difficult, especially when you're poor. The grandmother never gave up and always did what she could for her two grandchildren, but she paid a heavy price for all her efforts.

Over time, all the extra work required took a toll on the old lady. Fortunately, by then, the grandson, named David, went out and look for work. Some days, he earned enough to buy a bit of bread, but on others, work was scarce and because he was young and small, he often didn't get offered jobs.

Eventually, the grandmother's health declined, and as she became hungrier and thinner, it became more and more difficult for her to even get out of bed. David was desperate for money or a little bit of food but there seemed to be nothing that he could do.

One day, David heard of a dragon living in a cave in the mountains not far from his village. The Dragon was apparently large and fierce, and it had stolen a pot of gold from the King. The King was furious, and he had offered half of the pot of gold to any knight that could slay the dragon and retrieve the gold. From what David learned, there had been many knights who had accepted the challenge, and so far, the Dragon had defeated them all. David was fascinated by the story, or at least by the possibility of half a pot of gold, but he knew, as a small and weak boy, there was no way he would be a match for the Dragon.

Early one morning, as he was walking to town to look for work, he spied an old lady walking along the path ahead of him. On her shoulder, she carried a heavy bag, and when he got near to her, David offered to carry it for her. She was struggling, and she happily agreed to let the young man carry the heavy load. The bag was surprisingly heavy, but David didn't complain, and he carried it all the way to the edge of town where the old lady said that she would be going in a different direction to the one he was taking.

As he handed her back the bag, he apologized for not carrying it further and explained to her he needed to go into town to find work. The lady said that she didn't mind and thanked him profusely for all that he had done. After that, she reached into a pocket on her dress and pulled out a small bottle she handed it to him.

"This," she explained to the young boy, "is a magic sleeping potion. If you give it to someone or to some creature, it will make them sleep for at least a week. I don't have anything else to give you, but I hope that one day this tiny reward will pay you back for helping me with my load."

David didn't know what to do with the bottle, but he was grateful that he had helped the old lady and so he slipped it into his pocket and continued on his way to the village. It was a hot day, and he sat in the village square until midday, but nobody wanted to offer him work. While he was sitting there, a knight rode into the village on a great white horse. The man was wearing shining armor, and he carried a giant shield. On his belt hung a vicious looking sword. Soon all the villagers were talking about him, and from what David gathered, the knight tried to overcome the Dragon and gain his reward.

David decided to wait in town and see whether the knight succeeded and not. There was no point in rushing home as he had no food to take to either his sister or his ailing grandmother. Soon the knight left town, heading up into the hills where the great Dragon was rumored to live. David had assumed that it would take many hours before he returned. Surely a battle with a large Dragon must be a long and slow process. Instead, the knight returned after less than an hour. He was looking harassed and tired, and his horse was covered in black soot. Clearly, the Dragon had gotten the better of both. Discouraged and beaten, the knight rode out of town, shaking his head.

Although the sight of them in such a state was shocking, it caused David to think. He wondered if there was any way he could sneak some of the magic potions that the old lady had given him into the Dragon's food. If the potion were as strong as she had suggested, then perhaps the Dragon would fall asleep long enough to allow David to steal into the cave and come away with the famous pot of gold.

It was a bold and desperate idea. But David knew that he was in a desperate state and had nothing to lose. Without waiting any longer – in case he lost his nerve – he headed straight up the track that the knight had just ridden down. Soon the town was far behind him, and as he wound up the narrow path, the forest became denser and denser until the shadows made it almost dark. David was becoming very nervous, but he didn't allow himself to think about what could go wrong. Instead, he focused on what he would do with the pot of gold if he obtained it. The path continued to climb even more steeply, and eventually, just when he was on the point of giving up, he saw the mouth of a deep cave.

He could see nothing inside the darkness, but he was sure this was the home of the dreaded Dragon. Quietly, David crept up to the edge of the cave and peered inside. It was so dark he could see nothing, but he could hear the deep, steady rumble of something breathing. Now he was convinced this was the home of the Dragon that has stolen the gold from the King. David wondered how he could possibly trick the Dragon into taking some of the magic potion that the old lady had given him. He moved back from the entrance to the cave and sat down on the grass to think. He noticed that above the cave was an apple tree, and in front of the cave was a pile of apple cores almost the size of a small hill.

David wondered if he coated an apple with the magic potion, whether he could tempt the Dragon to eat it. He looked around in the grass they he spotted a shiny red apple. He lifted up the tiny bottle from his pocket and poured some of the potion onto the skin of the apple. He had to be very careful not to drop the potion on himself in case it made him go to sleep. After that, he threw the apple carefully in front of the entrance to the cave, and then he hid behind a tree and waited to see what would happen.

It was a full hour before David finally heard movement in the cave. Shortly after that, the giant Dragon dragged himself out of the cave entrance, where he spotted the apple lying on the ground. The Dragon sniffed the apple cautiously and, for a second, David worried that it might detect the potion he had painted on it. Instead, the Dragon picked up the apple in one of his clawed hands and then sat down and munched it.

After that, things happened quite quickly. The Dragon gave a mighty yawn and then turned around and went back into the cave. Just a few minutes later, the sound of heavy snoring could be heard coming out of the cave. David was nervous, but he knew that now was his only chance, and so he crept forward to the edge of the cave. Peering inside, he could just make out the form of the giant Dragon curled up in a ball at the back of the cave.

On tiptoes, David crept into the cave, ready to turn and run at a moment's notice. All the while, the Dragon was snoring loudly. Right at the back of the cave, David spotted a container. He moved up to it, and sure enough, it was the pot of gold that had attracted the attention of so many knights over the years. It took all of David's strength, but he dragged that pot out of the cave and back down the hill to the village he had come from. All the while, the sound of the Dragon snoring continued.

When David presented the pot of gold to the King, the king could not believe his eyes. He had watched dozens of knights over the years as they sought to fight the Dragon, and now, he was being presented with his gold by a small boy. The king was so impressed with David's courage he not only gave him half the pot of gold as a reward, but he also presented him with a house in the village much more comfortable than the one in which his sister and grandmother were living.

When David returned home to his sick grandmother with a pile of gold and news of his adventure, she could hardly believe what she was hearing. For David's part, he was so tired after his journey up the mountain and sneaking up on the giant Dragon he was asleep almost before he could finish telling her of his great adventure.

Chapter 15: Remington the Seagull

Remington was a seagull, and, like all seagulls, he liked to follow fishing boats and pick up scraps that the fishermen threw away. Remington was a very popular seagull, and he lived with a flock of other seagulls in the small fishing port. Each morning the seagulls would watch the fishing boats go out, and then they would pick one and follow it as it cruised out to sea, looking for a catch.

The problem was seagulls have no way of telling the difference between a fishing boat and the other boats that would regularly leave the harbor. One day Remington and his friends followed a boat from the harbor that was a pirate boat and not a fishing boat at all. Fishermen don't mind being followed by seagulls, and they happily share parts of the catch with the birds that follow the boat. Pirates, on the other hand, hate seagulls and, on this occasion, it was a pirate boat that the seagulls had chosen to follow.

Of course, the birds had no way of knowing this, and they just followed the boat, hoping to pick up something to eat. When they moved a little closer to see what was happening on the deck, the pirates quickly became annoyed at the presence of these noisy birds. One of them reached down and picked up a piece of metal lying on the deck, and as the seagulls grew closer, he hurled it into the flock of birds. The piece of metal spun through the air and smashed into Remington's wing.

Remington hadn't even seen the piece of metal coming, and the first time he learned of it was when he felt a sharp pain in his left-wing. Remington was a young bird, and the attack was unexpected. All his life, he had associated boats with food.

The piece of metal that had been thrown at him broke his wing, and Remington spun through the air and then crashed into the water. The pain was bad, but worse still was that now Remington couldn't fly. He paddled among the waves with his feet, but even though he tried, he could not take off again.

For a seagull, being unable to fly would spell death. Seagulls need to travel great distances to get to the food, and with a broken wing, it would just be a matter of time before Remington starved to death or was spotted by a shark and eaten alive. Remington's friends understood the danger that he was in, and they landed in the water nearby to try to help and encourage him.

"Don't worry, Remington, we will look after you," the other birds told him. "We will take turns in bringing you food."

It was a kind and generous offer, but both the Remington and the other seagulls knew there was little chance he could survive with a broken wing. All floated on the water, looking gloomy and wishing there was something that they could do. It was while they were floating there that a mermaid suddenly popped up from the deep amongst them.

The mermaid, named Cindy, took one look at Remington and knew there was a serious problem. She carefully lifted the injured bird, and then, swimming on the surface, took him to a small beach on an island not far from where the attack had taken place. When she got him there, she collected some seaweed and carefully bound his broken wing. After that, she found food for him and began to cautiously nurse him back to health.

It was many months before Remington could fly again and he and Cindy became the closest of friends. Every morning she would change the seaweed on the wounded wing before swimming out to sea to catch fish for the bird to eat. In the evenings, when she slept among the rocks, Remington would sleep cuddled up at her side, safe knowing that the mermaid would protect him from any predators.

Eventually, the wing healed, and it was no longer necessary to bind it with seaweed in the mornings. Slowly at first, Remington stretched and exercised the wing, and eventually, he took short flights. After that, the flights became longer and longer until finally, he flew as well as he could before the injury.

When Remington, at last, caught up with all his friends, they could not believe how healthy he was looking and how well he was able to fly. Although it was nice for Remington to return to his family and friends, he had become very close to Cindy the mermaid, and he would often seek her out on the island and spend the day with his new friend.

Mermaids are shy creatures, and they don't make friends very easily, but Cindy was always glad when Remington was able to take time to join her. Often, the bird and the mermaid would lie in the warm sand together, side-by-side in the afternoon sun. They couldn't talk to one another, but that didn't seem to harm the friendship. With the sun gently warming their bodies in the sand beneath them, the pair were happy to just be with one another and lie side-by-side. Often, they became so comfortable that the two would just doze off and sleep quietly on the beach.

Chapter 16: The Mermaid's Tears

There was once a pirate who came to believe that pearls were made from mermaid's tears. He was so passionate about this idea that he set out to capture a mermaid hoping she could make his fortune.

There is no truth in the rumor that pearls are made from mermaid's tears. The pirate was not clever enough to know that. He was sure that if he caught a mermaid, then all he would have to do would be to make her cry, and he could become one of the richest men in the world.

Gathering his men, he steered his ship out of the harbor and toward a small island where mermaids were said to live. The island was many miles from the harbor because mermaids are shy creatures, and they don't stay where there are people. It took several days for the pirate ship to reach the island, and when it did, they sailed around and around while the pirate peered through his telescope, looking for signs of mermaids.

After many days of not spotting a mermaid, the pirate and his crew were about to give up and go home. That was when one man, sitting in the crow's nest right at the top of the mast, suddenly shouted that he could see a mermaid lying on some rocks on the edge of the island.

Immediately, the pirate changed course and headed in the direction that the sailor was pointing.

There was a mermaid laying on the rocks, but as soon as she spotted the ship coming toward her, she slipped into the water and vanished for a few minutes. Although the crew had lost sight of the prey, they knew that the mermaid would have to come up for air sooner or later. The pirate ordered all hands on deck, and all the sailors peered into the sea hoping to catch sight of the mermaid.

Several minutes later, the mermaid poked her head above the surface to take a breath. She was quickly spotted by one of the crew, and the pirate changed course again to head in her direction. Once more, the mermaid dived, and once again, the sailors all scanned the water to see where she would come up. The hunt continued for over an hour. Time after time, the mermaid popped up for air, and each time the ship turned to follow her.

The problem was that the mermaid was getting tired, and each time she dived, she stayed down for a little less time. This made it easier for the boat to get close to her and harder and harder for her to escape. Finally, it was too much for the poor mermaid. She rose to the surface, desperate for air, and before she could go down again, one sailor dived into the water and grabbed her firmly around the waist. The crew threw a rope down to him, and soon the exhausted mermaid was hauled out of the water and dropped onto the deck of the ship.

"Ah-ha," cried the pirate. "Now, I shall have my pearls. You are going to make me rich, you pretty little thing."

If the pirate thought it would be difficult to make the mermaid cry, he was mistaken. Tired and frightened, she burst into tears almost as soon as he had spoken. This delighted the pirate until he realized that her tears were the same as anyone else's and there were no pearls appearing. The pirate was furious.

"Where are the pearls?" he yelled. "Your tears are supposed to become pearls. What's wrong with you?"

The poor mermaid had no idea what he was talking about, and all his anger did was make her more afraid and even more tearful. No matter how much she cried, there was no sign of those tears becoming pearls.

Angrier than ever, the pirate was not sure what to do with his prisoner. He had wasted days hunting her, and now he wanted to see some return for all his effort. Finally, he decided that if he couldn't make her produce tears that turned to pearls, then he would take her back to the harbor and try to sell her. Perhaps, he thought to himself, a zoo would be interested in having a mermaid as one of its attractions.

The frightened mermaid was helpless to do anything but lie on the deck and tremble as the boat turned and pointed its nose towards the harbor it had come from. It was while she was lying there that the mermaid spotted a seagull high in the sky above the boat. She didn't recognize him at that distance, but as the bird came a little lower, she knew that this was a seagull named Remington, who she had once helped when he had a broken wing.

From his lofty position in the sky, the sharp-eyed Remington could see that the mermaid on the deck was called Cindy. She had become his friend when these same pirates had broken his wing by throwing a piece of metal at him. Remington hated the pirates, and as soon as he saw his friend on the deck, he knew that he had to help. The only question was how a small seagull could take on a whole ship full of pirates. He made a low pass over the ship, calling out in his harsh seagull voice as he did so. He knew that though the mermaid wouldn't understand what he was saying, she would know that he had seen her. Remington hoped this would give her courage while he came up with a plan.

After that, Remington turned and headed back toward the harbor where he was soon surrounded by his many seagull friends. Quickly and desperately, he explained to them what the position was with the trapped mermaid. Since the attack on Remington, the seagulls had learned to spot a pirate boat, but now they feared it and always stayed well clear in case one of the pirates should throw something and injure another bird.

Though the birds were afraid, they all knew that they had to go to the help of the mermaid and try to get her away from the pirates. They also knew this was their chance to pay her back for looking after and nursing their friend Remington.

As one, the whole flock of seagulls took to the air and followed Remington as he led them toward the pirate ship. They didn't have a real plan, and they knew that they were just seagulls, but that didn't make them any less determined.

They soon reached the pirate ship and, without hesitation, followed Remington as he began to fearlessly dive-bomb the men on the boat. The pirates had never been attacked by seagulls before and were taken completely by surprise. Suddenly, bird after bird dive-bombed them, and the men were forced to duck for cover. The captain was steering the ship from behind the wheel, and he was very exposed to the angry seagulls. One after another, seagulls flashed past his head, giving it a kick or peck if they were given the slightest opportunity. Each time that happened, the captain had to duck, and the boat went further and further off course.

It was a situation the pirates were unprepared for. One minute they were sailing happily toward the harbor, and the next, they were being bombarded by clouds of angry seagulls. The gulls were screaming at them, pecking them, and even pooping on them. The pirate ship veered from side to side as the captain tried to avoid the dive-bombing seagulls.

Amidst this chaos, Cindy, the mermaid, slipped to the edge of the boat and drop into the water. The pirates didn't even notice her escape. Remington and the seagulls had noticed, however, but that didn't stop them from continuing to bombard the pirates. To tell you the truth, they were actually finding this quite fun.

They kept up the attack for quite a while, and by the time they decided that the pirates had had enough, the boat and its crew were white with seagull droppings. It would be another hour before the smelly ship finally made it back to the harbor. At about the same time, Remington was landing on the island beside his friend Cindy, the mermaid. He would spend the night with her and make sure that she slept safely and soundly after her terrible ordeal.

Chapter 17: The Dragon Zoo

There was once a powerful magician who collected dragons he placed in cages in a large zoo. He collected dragons, and people would pay large sums of money to come and see all the different species he had collected.

Although for the magician, this was a profitable business, it was terrible for the Dragons. Dragons are creatures used to being free, and they become very sad when confined to cages. They become even sadder when day after day they have people peering in and staring at them.

People have always feared dragons, and when word got around that the magician collected caged dragons, there was always a high demand to see them. Most people had always assumed dragons were all dangerous, fire-breathing creatures. They were always surprised when they discovered that they were very few types of Dragon that could actually breathe fire and were dangerous. Most dragons are small, harmless creatures that are shy.

Every week or so, the magician would attach a cart to two very large ox. He would then drive the cart high into the mountains in search of dragons for the zoo. He had a simple trick for catching dragons. The magician had a magic potion which, when placed on a dragon's food and eaten quickly, put the Dragon into a deep, deep sleep. Then the magician would haul the sleeping Dragon up onto the cart and take it back to his zoo. By the time the Dragon woke up, he would already be caged behind steel bars.

Each morning the Dragons would curl up and hide at the back of their cages to try and get a little privacy from the prying eyes focused on them throughout the day. At night, when the zoo was closed, the only sound you could hear would be that of sad dragons sobbing.

One dragon that sobbed himself to sleep every night was a small Dragon named Claude. Until he was captured by the wizard, Claude had lived a happy life with his two parents high in the mountains. There he would spend the day playing with his friends or with his mother and father. When news reached his parents that their son had been captured, they were devastated.

Claude's mother had been hearing rumors of dragons going missing for many years but had never imagined that her son Claude would be one of the missing. She refused to just accept that her son was gone forever. Instead, she searched high and low for him. Day after day, she would wander through the hills and forests and look for her son. Every creature she came across, she would question in case she could find news of Claude's whereabouts.

Once, when she was out searching among the woods, she came across Raven. When she questioned him as to whether he had seen a dragon, Raven told her of the dragon zoo in the village at the foot of the mountains. Although Claude's mother was shocked by the news, at least she knew now where her son was, and she made a plan to get him back again.

She gathered together many dragons and told them of the zoo that Raven had mentioned. Many of these dragons had also lost friends and family, and they were shocked to hear about the zoo. They all realized that they needed to group together to free those captured dragons. The problem was, they didn't know what to do. The magician was rumored to be very powerful, and if they confronted him, he could cast a spell on any of them.

In the end, the meeting with the dragons got her nowhere. They were all just too scared of the magician to take any action. Claude's mother was so saddened that all she could do was crawl back to her cave and sob. Even though her husband tried to comfort her, Claude's mother continued to cry all night.

There is something that you need to understand about dragon tears. They are very big and very wet. Unbeknown to Claude's parents, for years they had been sharing their cave with a tiny mouse, and all the tears were pouring into his mouse hole and making him wet.

Suddenly Claude's parents were disturbed by a tiny indignant voice.

"Hey, would you stop all of that crying. You are flooding my house."

The two dragons looked at one another. Who was this tiny, bedraggled-looking creature that was shouting at them despite his tiny size?

"I'm sorry," Claude's mother said. "I didn't mean to make you wet."

The mouse sighed.

"What is so bad that it is making you cry so much and flood my house anyway?" he asked.

"A wizard has stolen our son and is keeping him in a zoo at the foot of the mountains," Mrs. Dragon answered.

"Well, why don't you go down there and get him back?" asked the mouse. "At least that way, I might be able to get some sleep."

"It's not quite as easy as that," explained Claude's father. "The magician is very powerful, and he could cast a spell on us. What is more, none of the other dragons will help us."

"Oh, dear," said the grumpy little mouse. "I suppose that I will have to help you. Take me down to this zoo, and I will see what I can do."

The two dragons looked at one another. Who was this tiny little creature that was so fearless, and how could he help?

"Come on, come on," snapped the mouse. "I haven't got all day, and I am in desperate need of sleep."

Soon after that, the two dragons were heading down the mountain with the tiny mouse riding on Claude's father's back. It was a long way to the village, and it was getting dark when they finally reached it. On the outskirts lay a fenced area with a big sign, *Dragon Zoo*. As they got closer, the mouse gave further orders.

"You better hang about here out of sight. I'll go and check out what is happening."

With that, the fearless mouse clambered down from Mr. Dragon's back and waddled toward the zoo. He was gone a very long time, and the dragons were forced to sit in the forest at the edge of the village and just wait for his return.

It was very dark, and the dragons heard the mouse before they saw him. In fact, what they heard did not sound like a mouse. It was a metallic clinking sound that at first neither of them could identify. They peered into the darkness, and finally, they could just make out the little mouse pulling something behind him.

"Well, you could at least give a hand," snapped the mouse when he got near enough to talk to them.

The dragons stepped forward, and they eventually made out what the mouse had been struggling with. It was a large ring of keys. Mr. Dragon could pick it up easily, but it had taken a great deal of effort for the mouse to drag it all the way from the zoo.

"There you go. Those are the keys to the zoo. They were too heavy for me to drag up to the locks, but you will easily be able to manage."

The dragons were amazed, and *for* a second, they just stared at the mouse.

"Get going then," ordered the mouse. "You don't have long before it gets light, and you will want to be clear of here by then."

The dragons turned and dashed toward the zoo.

"Don't forget to pick me up before you head back up the mountain," a tiny voice shouted out to them as they left.

Quietly, the dragons let themselves into the zoo using the keys the mouse had stolen. There, they were confronted with row after row of cages, and they moved from one to another and letting the captive dragons out. As Claude's father unlocked the cages, his mother went ahead, trying to locate the cage that her son was in. As she went, she kept calling out his name.

"Claude, Claude," she called. "Where are you?" At each cage, she would ask if the dragon inside had seen her son and then tell the dragon inside that her husband would be along shortly with the keys to release them. None had seen Claude, and his mother was becoming frantic.

Finally, she turned a corner and saw her son huddled in the back of a tiny cage. She was in tears by then, and she held her son's hand as they waited for his dad to come and open the cage.

By the end of the rescue, over thirty dragons were released, and they poured out of the zoo and went back up toward the mountains and forests where they had lived before the magician had captured them.

Claude and his family could not go straight home. First, they had to return to the spot where they had left the brave little mouse. They found him sound asleep beneath a dry leaf where they might not have seen him had he not been snoring so loudly.

Mrs. Dragon placed him on her back for the journey home while Mr. Dragon carried Claude. Both the mouse and the young dragon slept soundly for the whole journey. When they finally reached their cave, the dragons placed their sleeping son in his bed and then very gently lowered the snoring mouse back into his tiny hole, which had fortunately dried out by then. Neither of them would wake up for several hours.

Chapter 18: The Elf and The Princess

Princess Anna was a spoiled girl. First, she was a princess, but she was also an only child and the apple of the king's eye.

She had every toy you could imagine. She also had three ponies, two dogs, and a small mini palace that even had a moat going around it. Because she was spoiled and she was never disciplined, Princess Anna was very naughty. She would never listen to her nanny nor the maids, and she even ignored the queen. Occasionally she would listen to her father, the king, but because he was so fond of her, and because he was often away overseeing his kingdom, he would seldom discipline her when he ought to have.

The result of this bad behavior was that Anna was very unpopular with the staff at the palace. None of the workers at the royal household wanted to have anything to do with the young princess, and they would avoid working for her. As for the palace staff, looking after the princess was a job they considered punishment.

Princess Anna didn't care about the staff. She liked to do her own thing, and she knew that at the end of the day, because she was a princess, everyone would have to do what she told them to do even if they didn't like it. The problem with the situation was that the Royal staff avoided the Princess and, as a result, she often found herself alone when there ought to be somebody there to attend to her.

This became bad at night when she could not sleep. Normally, if a princess couldn't sleep, there would be a maid in waiting who could fetch a glass of milk and perhaps read her a story until she was ready to doze off. Often in Anna's case, maids would have sneaked off somewhere to keep well clear of the princess. Anna might wake up to find herself all alone and with no one to help her.

It was on one occasion when she found herself wide awake during the night that Anna wandered about in the palace gardens. The palace was walled and heavily guarded, so there was no question of her being in any danger. All the same, she found it quite frightening to be wandering among the huge trees, hedges, and flower beds that made up the magnificent gardens of the palace. There were dark shadows, and the night was filled with strange noises, and even though in her mind she knew she was safe, Princess Anna became quite afraid.

As she became more and more uncomfortable in the dark, she decided that she would return to the comfort of her bed, even though she was still wide awake. As she turned to head for home, she spotted a small figure darting across the pathway ahead of her. In her mind, it looked like an elf, but she was convinced that elves did not really exist and that they were just stories that people made up in old folk tales.

Princess Anna was not sure what to do now. Had she imagined this tiny figure, and should she just continue home and pretend she had never seen it? She was surer now than ever that she could not sleep when she reached her bed. As the path ahead became still again, she convinced herself that what she had seen did not exist and was just her imagination. Slowly she moved forward. As soon as she moved, she noticed the small figure scurrying ahead of her again.

Anna was torn between being frightened and being angry. She was a princess. Who was this tiny creature scurrying around in her palace gardens in the middle of the night?

"Who are you?" she shouted, trying to sound braver than she really was.

The small figure stopped running and turned around. Cautiously, the princess moved toward the creature, who stood calmly waiting for her. As she drew closer, the princess knew that this was one of the legendary elves she had heard about. The elf seemed unconcerned to be in the presence of a royal princess.

"Who are you, and what are you doing in my garden?" demanded the princess, trying to sound far more confident than she felt.

"My name is Murdoch, the elf."

"Well, I am Princess Anna, and what are you doing in my garden?"

"I know very well who you are," said the elf. "You are the spoiled little princess that everybody speaks about. As far as I'm concerned, this garden is as much mine as it is yours. My ancestors have been living here for over a thousand years, and I am not about to be too pushed around by a grumpy little princess."

The princess was shocked. She was not accustomed to anybody speaking back to her, and certainly not to anyone telling her she was spoiled.

"How dare you speak to me like that," she snapped. "Don't you know that with just one word to the king, I could have your head removed?"

The elf didn't even look remotely frightened. Instead, he made a sort of humph noise.

"Oh, please," he sighed. "After a thousand years of living side-by-side with you humans, do you really think that we are the least bit afraid of you?"

"Well, you'd better be. I am a royal princess, and I will not be talked to like that by anyone, least of all by a tiny little elf."

"Well, I see that the rumors about you being a spoiled and bossy little girl are absolutely true," said Maddock. "I think perhaps it is about time somebody taught you some manners, and clearly none of the palace staff are going to do that. It looks like the job is going to fall to me." With that, the elf clicked his tiny fingers, and instantly, the princess shrank to a size that was no bigger than he was.

The Princess gasped. Suddenly, from being a normal-sized princess, she found herself as a tiny creature not too dissimilar to the one standing in front of her.

"How dare you!" she yelled in a new and tiny voice. "I am a royal princess, and I will not be treated like this."

"Well, actually, your royal highness, it's too late. You have already been treated like this. In fact, if you continue to behave so badly, I will see to it that you are treated far worse. Right now, I think it's time you started learning by doing some chores so that you get a better understanding of what life is like for ordinary people."

With that, the elf turned on his heels and walked into the woods. The princess stood and watched him disappear among the trees.

"What are you doing just standing there?" he asked as soon as he realized that she wasn't following him. "Come on, girl, follow me and hurry up."

"I will not follow you. Who do you think you are?"

The little elf didn't hesitate for a second. He gave a click of his fingers, and instantly a large wart grew on the side of the princess's nose. Princess Anna was horrified, and she gave a startled cry.

"Unless you want to find yourself covered in warts from head to toe, it might be an idea for you to start listening to my orders more quickly," snapped Maddock.

Princess Anna was too shocked to argue, and as the elf turned and continued on his way, she scurried after him, fearful that he might punish her with another wart. They had not gone far when they came to a small door in the base of a giant oak tree. Anna had seen that big tree often before but had never noticed the tiny door at its base. Maddock opened the door and stepped into the tiny room that occupied the inside of the oak tree. For a moment, Anna hesitated, but then she too stepped through the door and found herself in a tiny cozy little house she would never have known existed.

"You see that fireplace over there?" he asked, pointing to the hearth. "It needs to be cleaned out, and after that, you'll need to go and look for firewood and get the fire going so that you can make dinner."

Now Anna was becoming annoyed. She was a princess, and she was not at all accustomed to being told what to do or being told to do chores that were fit only for a servant.

"I most certainly will not," she replied. "I am a princess of the highest order, and that is a job for a servant."

The little elf didn't hesitate for a second. He gave a quick flick of his fingers, and instantly the princess felt another wart grow on the side of her nose. Slowly it was dawning on the princess she was no longer in control. This elf didn't care whether or not she was a princess, and for the first time in her life, Anna realized that she had absolutely no choice.

With great difficulty, because she was unaccustomed to doing chores, the princess set about cleaning the hearth. To her disgust, she discovered that it was hard and dirty work, and soon her lovely pink nightdress was smeared with soot and coal dust. She had no choice but to continue lest the elf placed another wart on her face. The princess had always prided herself on her beauty, and the appearance of these warts was devastating to her.

Once she had cleaned out the fireplace, the elf dispatched her into the forest to gather wood and kindling, which he then forced her to use to light a fire. Never having lit a fire before, Anna found the whole job to be far more difficult than she had imagined. Twice, her attempt at a fire went out, and Maddock shouted at her. On the third occasion, she burst into tears, and the elf took pity on her and finally lit the fire himself.

When the fire was blazing, the elf placed a pot of soup over the flames to start warming. It was not the sort of food that the princess was accustomed to but, by then, the cold of the night, and her unfamiliar efforts had made her tired and hungry. She looked forward to the soup more than she thought she would. The problem was that it was not for her.

As soon as the soup was bubbling in its pot, the elf picked up a bowl and served himself a large helping. Anna sat and watched as he began to eat and then asked if there was any for her.

"This fine food is not for servants," said Maddock indignantly. "Do your maids and servants eat the same fine food and cake that you have on your table? I don't think so. In fact, I suspect that you are such a spoiled little princess that you have no idea what your servants eat."

The elf continued to sip at his hot soup, and Anna could do only stand by and watch with her mouthwatering. For the first time in her life, she realized that what he said was correct. She had no idea what her maids and the other palace servants ate. All she knew was that she always had the finest of fare placed before her.

When the elf had finished eating, he handed Anna the bowl to wash. Only when she had washed it and placed it back in his tiny cupboard did he hand her a piece of dry bread to chew on. It was stale and horrible but, by then, the princess was so hungry that she ate it anyway.

As she sat in the corner, chewing on the dry crust of bread, tears formed in Anna's eyes. She missed the wonderful cakes she would have been served in the palace; she missed the warm milk she could have ordered any time, and above all, she missed the comfort and warmth that a cozy bed would have provided if she hadn't got up that night.

The elf turned and watched her, and she tried to hide her tears.

"I think," he said, "that it's perhaps time for me to take you home. I hope that tonight's little adventure has taught you to be a kinder and more considerate person."

With that, the elf opened the door and went back out into the dark woods. This time Anna didn't hesitate for a second. She followed him immediately, desperately hoping that he would take her back to the palace.

The sun was beginning to lighten on the horizon when, eventually, the tiny elf brought her to the doors of the palace. He turned and looked at her for a long time, and she stood in front of him feeling fearful but also a little ashamed. She understood now that many people lived different lives to the privileged life she lived. For the first time in her life, she understood just how spoiled she was and how lucky she had always been.

"Well, my young Princess," said Maddock with a slight smile on his face, the first she had seen since she met him. "I suspect that tonight has been quite a learning experience for you. I hope that in the future, you take a kinder approach to the people that work for you."

"Oh, I will, I will," she promised sincerely.

"In that case, I shall bid you good night," and with that, the tiny elf turned on his heel and walked away.

"What about my warts...and my size?" The princess sounded quite desperate.

"Oh dear, I almost forgot about that," said Maddock. He turned back toward the Princess, and this time he really was smiling. It was quite a nice smile, and Anna couldn't help but smile back at him even though she was desperate to be turned back into her former self. Maddock gave two quick clicks of his fingers, and Anna was transformed back into the beautiful princess she had always been. Even her nightdress, once black with coal dust, was clean again. She couldn't help but rub her nose with her fingers just to make sure that the warts were no longer there.

She watched for a few seconds as Maddock disappeared into the shadows, and then she let herself into the palace and slipped upstairs into her room. She promised herself that never again would she take her maid or the other servants for granted. Even as she was drifting off to sleep and the bed was reaching that deep, cozy warm temperature it does just before you fall asleep, she gently rubbed the edge of her nose just to make sure that her warts had gone away.

Chapter 19: The Plain Princess

Many years ago, high in the mountains, was a kingdom known as the Golden Kingdom. It was governed by a very popular king whose people loved him much. The king had no sons, but he did have three daughters. Their names were Charlotte, Ariel, and Constance.

Ariel and Constance were younger than their sister, and they were both very beautiful. As they grew older, they were frequently courted by rich young men and the princes of the kingdom. Charlotte, who would one day become heir to the throne, was regrettably plain.

When they were young, Charlotte was unaware of her lack of beauty. As they became older, however, the attention that her two younger sisters garnered became more and more obvious. For years, Charlotte tried to ignore this problem and pretend that all was well. Unfortunately, as she started to become a young woman, the fact that all the young men in the kingdom preferred her sisters really hurt her.

The king, unfortunately, did not understand. He thought that because Charlotte would one day be the queen of the kingdom that would make up for the fact that she wasn't as beautiful as her two younger sisters. Not only were her sisters more beautiful than she was, but they were also far more confident and outgoing and were forever being invited to parties, picnics and balls. While they were away,

Charlotte would find herself alone at the palace, where she spent most of her time reading or wandering in the palace gardens.

Although she was decidedly plain-looking, Charlotte was definitely a favorite among the palace staff. Ariel and Constance were self-centered and vain. Charlotte, on the other hand, was kind and gentle, and those who worked for her appreciated her nicer nature.

Charlotte's mother had died shortly after the birth of her third daughter. Charlotte often wondered if she'd been able to talk to her mother and explain her problems if her mother could have guided her as to what she should do. She loved the King dearly, but he was a man, and he didn't seem to appreciate the pain she was feeling because of being much less beautiful than her sisters.

Charlotte had a handmaid named Mary. She was an old woman who had been the handmaid of her mother before she had died. She was probably the person to whom Charlotte was closest. Mary watched with concern as she saw how unhappy the princess had become. Charlotte ate less and lose weight but, more important, Mary knew that she wasn't sleeping properly and would often spend the night wandering through the palace or reading books by the light of a candle.

Charlotte's lack of sleep worried Mary more than anything else. The old maid was wise, and she knew from experience that sleep was important. Sleep could keep the mind from being troubled, the heart from being sore, and the body from being wary. Mary would often talk to Charlotte about her problems, but she seemed unable to reassure Charlotte that, over time, her looks would cease to be important. If she became a beloved queen in the way that her father was loved by the people, it would be her kindness and gentle nature that would have to shine through. Mary was old enough to know that beautiful looks were just like a passing shadow and that they would not last forever. Kindness would be something that would last Con Charlotte stance for the rest of her life.

Eventually, Mary became so concerned about Princess Charlotte she arranged for her to visit a witch named Theodora the wise. Mary had to be careful about this arrangement because she knew that the king would not be happy if he knew that the princess was consulting with witches. Mary also knew that Theodora was a very, very wise woman and not a harmful witch like so many others were.

Theodora, the wise, lived in a small cottage even higher up the mountains than the palace was. Mary had to devise an excuse to take Charlotte to her in a manner that would not arouse the suspicions of the King. What Mary did was wait until the two younger princesses had been invited to one of their many parties, and then she took Charlotte on a picnic. She knew that the king would accept this excuse, and he would not know that they just visited the wise witch while they were out.

Mary carefully packed a large basket with all the food, treats, and drinks that one would expect to take on a picnic. She took a blanket for them to sit on and was also careful to include gifts for the wise witch. Once she had gathered all that they needed, she called Charlotte and led her up a narrow winding path that took them into the mountains where the witch's cottage was. It was a long journey, and the climb was very steep. All the way, Charlotte kept asking Mary where they were going and why they had to go so far just for a picnic. All Mary could do was tell her to be patient and that sooner or later, all would be revealed.

It took well over an hour until they finally left the steep path and step into a small clearing in which stood a tiny wooden cottage. Mary was relieved there was smoke trickling from the chimney as this assured her that the witch was home. Leading the way, Mary walked up to the door and gave a gentle knock.

The door was opened by a tiny wizened old lady, at least a foot shorter than Charlotte. Mary introduced the young princess, but it was clear that Theodora already knew who she was.

"You are the oldest princess who will one day be queen," she said.

"Yes, I am, but how did you know that?" asked Charlotte.

"Oh, I may be old and nearly blind, but Theodora sees many things that normal people cannot see," she said in a tiny crackling voice that Charlotte found quite charming.

Theodora led them into the tiny cottage and offered the maid and the princess seats next to a small fire over which hung a cauldron of delicious-smelling soup.

"What brings you two ladies all the way up from the royal palace to my tiny little cottage?" asked Theodora.

Mary had never explained to Charlotte she was bringing the princess up to see the wise witch to consult her about her plain looks, and so Charlotte was a little baffled herself as to why they were there.

"Princess Charlotte has two very beautiful sisters," explained Mary to the wise witch. "She worries that she gets much less attention from many of the young knights and princes and feels that her looks are far too plain. I was hoping that you would be able to convince our young princess how unimportant her beauty is and make her understand that it is her kindness and her gentle nature that are to be valued."

The old witch nodded and then moved close to the princess and peered carefully into her face. For a long time, she studied the princess, and Charlotte was beginning to feel uncomfortable at the close examination.

"I think you are wrong, Mary," said the old witch. "Beauty is very important, especially in someone who will one day be the most important queen in the land. But I also think what you are failing to see is the inner beauty that exists in Princess Charlotte. To be honest with you, I have seen many a fair maiden, and this young princess is the fairest of them all. The problem we have is that she has failed to recognize just how beautiful she is. What we need is a way to show Charlotte her own beauty and not a way to make her any more beautiful than she already is. I believe I have just the thing."

The old witch turned and opened a large wooden box that stood behind beside the fireplace. When they had first entered the cottage, Charlotte had thought it contained firewood, but now, even in the dull light, she could see that the box was full of potions, bottles, and jars and other things that the princess could not identify.

The witch dug into the bottom of the box, and from there, she produced a black velvet bag. She handed this to the Princess and told her to open it and take out what she found inside. Charlotte reached into the bag, feeling slightly nervous she did. What she found inside was a hand mirror with a beautiful golden frame and a handle decorated with mother-of-pearl.

"Now look into the mirror," ordered the witch.

Charlotte did as she was told and was amazed to see that the reflection looking back at her was that of a beautiful young woman. She could see that the woman was herself, but somehow her face had changed slightly, and she was no longer the plain princess she had always seen staring back at her from the many mirrors that hung on the walls of the palace. The reflection shocked and delighted the princess at the same time. Taking the mirror, she ran outside so she could see herself in the brighter light. She was afraid that outside when she looked at the mirror all, she would see was the plain reflection she had grown used over the years. To her delight, the image she looked at was as stunningly beautiful as it had been in the cottage.

"What have you done? Why do I look so beautiful when I see myself in this mirror?" she asked when she went back into the cottage.

"I have done nothing, my child. All I have done is hand you a mirror that enables you to see yourself as you really are. What you didn't understand is that the beauty of your sisters will fade in the same way as the petals of a rose are bound to do. What you possess, and what you have failed to recognize, is deep and permanent beauty that will not disappear as you grow old."

After that, she sat down to the picnic that Mary had prepared and the soup simmering over the fire. Mary and the wise Theodora chatted as they ate, but Charlotte was quiet as she pondered the information she had received from the old witch. She ate all that was put in front of her out of politeness, but she would far rather have taken another look at herself in the mirror.

When they had eaten, Mary and Charlotte prepared to return to the palace.

"You take this mirror with you," instructed the witch. "From now on, whenever you imagine yourself as being plain or unattractive, I want you to look into the mirror to remind yourself of who you really are and what the rest of the world sees."

Before the two could depart, Theodora took Mary aside and handed her a small bottle of potion.

"I can see by looking into her eyes that the child has not been sleeping properly. Every night slip two drops of this potion into her dinner, and she will sleep soundly," instructed Theodora. "Sleep will strengthen her morale and give her confidence, which will be important when she becomes queen."

When they got back to the palace, Mary did what the wise witch had instructed, and after that, Charlotte was never troubled by poor sleep again. The king never did discover their visit to the witch who lived high in the mountains. It is true he would not have been pleased, but he did recognize that his daughter was no longer sad. Soon princes, knights, and wealthy young men from all over the kingdom - and from other lands - called, each seeking the hand of the beautiful princess Charlotte.

It would be many years before she chose one prince to become a husband. When her father eventually died, Queen Charlotte was even more beloved by the people than the king had been. She was wise and fair, but more than anything, she was gentle and kind.

Just as the witch had predicted, the beauty of Ariel and Constance faded with age, and, the inner beauty that had always existed in Charlotte shined through more and more strongly. She would always be known as the Beautiful Queen.

Chapter 20: The Last of the Unicorns

Once, the unicorns used to live at peace alongside people. They shared the same valleys and mountains and forests, and there was never any trouble between them. Unicorns were timid and shy, but because they had become used to humans, they had grown to trust them.

And then, one day, a sad thing happened. One unicorn died, and a man walking through the grass found his horn. Instead of just leaving it there where it had fallen, he picked it up and took it home with him. It was a beautiful thing, and the man decided that he would try to carve it into something useful. He took out his pocketknife and started to carve, and he soon found that the horn was soft and carved like butter. Also, as he carved and shaped it, the horn became even more beautiful than it had been before. The man turned the horn into a pipe, and when he had carved, shaping, and polishing, the pipe was so beautiful that he offered it to the king.

The king saw the pipe and realized that he had never seen such a wonderful thing. He was so impressed that he rewarded the man who had carved it, and he gave him as much gold as the man would normally earn in a year. This was when things got bad. Humans, by nature, are greedy, and when the man who carved the pipe saw how large his reward was, he decided that perhaps he could find another horn and make another pipe.

He spent days wandering in the hills and valleys looking for unicorn horns, but he did not find a single one. What he did see though, were many unicorns. Eventually, he decided that as he couldn't find a unicorn, he would kill one and take its horn for himself. He was already a fine hunter, and the unicorns trusted humans, so it was easy for him to kill one with his bow and arrow. He quickly cut off its horn and returned to his home, where he once again began to carve.

This time he made two fine spoons from the horn. They were so delicately carved and so beautiful to look at that as soon as the king laid eyes on them, he gave the man a small sack of gold and ordered several more. For the unicorns, this was the start of a terrible time. The first man began to hunt them, but when they saw how rich he had become, other men also hunted unicorns for their horns.

The leader of the unicorns was a big stallion named Thunder. He summoned the unicorns to a meeting in one of the lowland valleys, and they discussed this new and terrible state of affairs. Soon they had agreed that humans could no longer be trusted, and so Thunder led his herd high into the mountains to where they were most steep and covered in thick forests and mist. There the unicorns have stayed for many generations. Each new generation tells their children how dangerous humans are and how greedy they can become. They make sure that the young know the danger from humans and that they should always hide from them.

Humans have not seen unicorns for many generations and have grown to believe that they don't exist. Over the years, they have become creatures of myth and fairy tales, and many people don't believe in them.

This was the case of a young girl called Cassandra. She had heard all about unicorns; in fact, she played with a plastic one in her bedroom. Still, she was smart enough to know that they were not real. And then one day, she went to visit her old grandfather, and at his house, she happened upon a spoon that was the most beautiful thing she had ever seen. She took it to her grandfather, and he told her it once belonged to his great grandfather and that he had carved it from the horn of a unicorn. The man told his granddaughter that a long time before he had been born, unicorns used to feed on the sweet grass of the valley at the back of his house.

Cassandra didn't really believe her grandfather and his old fairy tales, but as she had nothing better to do, she wandered into the field while the other grown-ups were talking about boring things.

At about the same time, a young unicorn named Epiticus was growing bored up in the mountains. He had heard the fierce legends that all the older unicorns told of the cruel humans lower down the slopes, but he was not sure if they were real or not. He often thought they were something that older unicorns spoke about to frighten the youngsters into staying close to home. He was curious and bored, and that is always a dangerous combination in any young creature. As the other unicorns wandered and grazed among the trees of the forest, Epiticus slipped away from the herd and headed down the mountain.

He had not intended to go far. He was just bored, and he did not believe in these fierce humans. As he moved down the mountain, however, he found that the forest became much thinner, and there were glades filled with the sweetest grass he had ever tasted. He wondered why the other unicorns didn't move down there so they could all enjoy the fine food he saw so much of.

Epiticus was just about to turn around and head back towards the high forest when he noticed a strange creature, the likes of which he had never seen before. At exactly the same moment, Cassandra looked up and found herself staring at one of the most beautiful animals she had ever seen in her life. The two youngsters stared at one another for several minutes, both wondering what to do.

Epiticus tossed his head a little bit, and the young girl smiled. The unicorn thought she looked nice, so he tossed his head again and moved a little closer. Cassandra was enchanted, and she too took a few steps forward. Eventually, the young unicorn and the young girl were face to face.

"Who are you?" asked Epiticus.

"My name is Cassandra," she answered. "Who are you?"

"I am called Epiticus. Are you a human being?" Epiticus thought it was probably impolite to ask such a question, but he couldn't help himself.

"Yes, of course, I am, silly," Cassandra laughed.

"Are you here to hunt me so that you can cut off my horn?" asked the young unicorn, feeling alarmed for the first time.

"No, of course not," Cassandra replied, feeling quite shocked. "I love unicorns and think that you are the most beautiful creatures on earth. Why would you think I could possibly harm you?"

Epiticus looked at the girl, and then he told her the horrible stories he had heard about humans and about how dangerous they were.

"That is just so untrue," said Cassandra. "Why would anyone want to harm a creature as gentle and handsome as you are?"

Just then, Cassandra remembered the spoon that her grandfather had shown her and his words it was made from the horn of a unicorn. The thought sent a chill down her spine, and she decided she had better not mention this to Epiticus.

The two youngsters chatted about other things for over an hour, but then they both realized that it was becoming late and that they would be in trouble if they didn't get back home soon.

As she came through the door of her grandfather's house, he looked up and laughed.

"Well, Cassandra. Did you see any unicorns?"

Cassandra looked at the spoon she had been admiring earlier.

"No, grandad," she replied. "You know those creatures are just a fairy tale."

When Cassandra was tucked in bed that night, she thought about a handsome white unicorn called Epiticus. The fact that she had seen him would always remain her secret. She would never see him for real again, but Cassandra was happy just to know that unicorns really did exist. In fact, a strange thing happened after that. Each night, as she lay with her eyes closed and began to enjoy the gentle warmth of her bed, a white unicorn would visit her in her dreams. She would see him at the far side of a green meadow, and as she breathed in and out, he would toss his head and let her know that he was there and that he would watch over her as she slept.

Here's another book by Peggie Langston that you might like

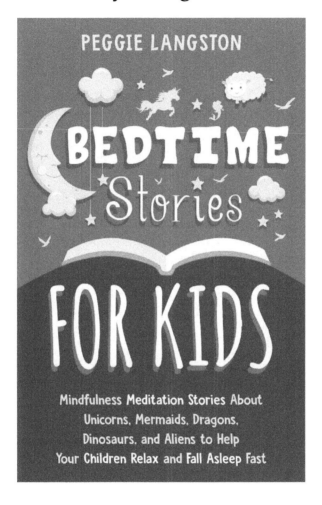

www.ingramcontent.com/pod-product-compliance
Lightning Source LLC
LaVergne TN
LVHW021452300125
802476LV00004B/707